HINDU RITES

and

RITUALS

Origins and Meanings

K.V. SINGH

PENGUIN BOOKS

PENGUIN BOOKS

Published by the Penguin Group

Penguin Books India Pvt. Ltd, 7th Floor, Infinity Tower C, DLF Cyber City, Gurgaon 122 002, Haryana, India

Penguin Group (USA) Inc., 375 Hudson Street, New York, New York 10014, USA

Penguin Group (Canada), 90 Eglinton Avenue East, Suite 700, Toronto, Ontario, M4P 2Y3, Canada

Penguin Books Ltd, 80 Strand, London WC2R 0RL, England

Penguin Ireland, 25 St Stephen's Green, Dublin 2, Ireland (a division of Penguin Books Ltd)

Penguin Group (Australia), 707 Collins Street, Melbourne, Victoria 3008, Australia

Penguin Group (NZ), 67 Apollo Drive, Rosedale, Auckland 0632, New Zealand

Penguin Books (South Africa) (Pty) Ltd, Block D, Rosebank Office Park, 181 Jan Smuts Avenue, Parktown North, Johannesburg 2193, South Africa

Penguin Books Ltd, Registered Offices: 80 Strand, London WC2R 0RL, England

First published by Penguin Books India 2015

Copyright © K.V. Singh 2015
Illustration copyright © Urmimala Nag 2015

10 9 8 7 6 5 4 3 2 1

The views and opinions expressed in this book are the author's own and the facts are as reported by him, which have been verified to the extent possible, and the publishers are not in any way liable for the same.

ISBN 9780143425106

Illustrations by Urmimala Nag
Typeset in Book Antiqua by Manipal Digital Systems, Manipal
Printed at Replika Press Pvt. Ltd, India

PENGUIN RANDOM HOUSE COMPANY

PENGUIN BOOKS

HINDU RITES AND RITUALS

Born in 1938, Lt Cdr K.V. Singh served in the armed forces for thirty years. He is widely travelled within the country and abroad, and has authored a number of books in English and Hindi, in addition to being an anchor and participant in numerous television programmes. He is currently the CEO of Flag Foundation of India.

This book is dedicated to those who are interested in Hinduism. In particular, the book is targeted at youths who are born in families with a Hindu heritage, but lead a life with a modern outlook, caring little for old values and traditions. The book will give them an insight into the soul of Hinduism.

Contents

Gods, Goddesses and Nature

Important Hindu Dates

Rituals: Pujas and *Yagnas*

Temple Rituals

Traditions

Miscellaneous

Preface

From a very early age, Hindus are introduced, and encouraged, to follow the various rules, rites, rituals and religious practices that seem to lie at the heart and soul of Hinduism. More often than not, these are blindly followed because our elders have been observing them and because we are told that we must follow them too. But most of us are unaware of the science behind the rites; there are logical explanations for all the dos and don'ts — we are simply not aware of them. Since no one has explained to us the rationale, the science and the logic that lies at the core of these religious practices, we are not to be blamed for our ignorance. Our parents, teachers and the pundits themselves are usually unaware of the truth. In the absence of appropriate knowledge about rituals, we conveniently call them superstitions without realizing our ignorance. Therefore, it is but a necessity that we understand the reasoning that guides the rituals and rites.

Most religions of the world came into being on account of the 'wonder' and 'fear' factors. Hinduism, however, had its genesis in questioning the existence of man: Who am I? Where did I come from? What is the aim of my life? Why was I born? Is there life beyond death? The ancient undiluted and unpolluted Sanatana religion was based on reasoning, the tool of modern science, and not on myth, as some may think. However, as time passed, people forgot the basic facts of Hinduism, and its rediscovery is useful for not just those who regard these rituals as meaningless but also for those who follow them unquestioningly.

Hindu rituals have two aspects — philosophical and scientific. We must understand them both to completely comprehend their true significance.

A sincere attempt has been made in this book to present hitherto unexplained facts about some of the rituals that are commonly followed by us in our day-to-day life, and the rationale behind each of them. It is hoped that readers will find these revelations enlightening and interesting, and take pride in what they do and why they practise those rituals.

It is also true that in this day and age of the Internet, with hectic lifestyles and instant gratification being the norm, most of the old traditions and rituals cannot be practised in the traditional way. Notwithstanding this unpleasant reality of modern age, a genuine effort may be made to unravel the principles behind these rituals, so as to follow them in their true spirit and not simply as a matter of tradition.

Introduction

What Makes India a Great Spiritual Land?

Since times immemorial, India has been the spiritual leader of the world. Four major religions—Hinduism, Jainism, Buddhism and Sikhism—were born here. Thousands of seers and saints have walked the length and breadth of this holy land and preached spirituality. Even today, when man's journey to the moon is a thing of the past and new boundaries in all fields are set and exceeded with impressive speed and confidence, the West looks towards India for inner peace. A natural question that comes up is: What makes India so great that economically advanced nations take spiritual refuge in India? Is it a mere coincidence that India has been the spiritual guru of the world or are there some veritable factors that make this subcontinent so sought after?

Great sages tell us that the foremost factor that contributes to India's spiritual greatness is its unique geo-location on this planet. India's natural locale is such that she receives certain exclusive divine vibrations and radiations together with the gravitational vim from

Jupiter and the sun. Astrologically, both these heavenly bodies are vital for the spiritual progress of human beings, and have played a significant role in the life of the people of India in making them spiritual in their outlook.

During ancient days, India was a land so serene and pure that Mother Nature was in perfect harmony here. The five principal elements or the *panchabhoota*s — earth, water, air, fire and ether — of which human beings are made, were fully balanced with the forces of nature, whose clock moved with perfect precision. The duration of each season was consistent, and the transition from one season to the other was smooth and timely. Life was simple and peaceful, without any stress or strain.

In addition, two mountain ranges, the Aravallis (the oldest) and the Himalayas (the youngest), both in India — a divine design rather than a coincidence — also impacted India's spiritual strength. Spiritually speaking, the Aravallis represent the *agni tatwa* or the fire element while the Himalayas the *jala tatwa* or the water element of Mother Nature. Most rishis and munis had their abode in the Himalayas and the Aravallis owing to the pull between the longitudes and latitudes of the two ranges, which is such that the agni tatwa and the jala tatwa are conducive for the spiritual growth of mankind.

The rivers of India — Ganga, Godavari, Yamuna, Sindhu, Saraswati, Kaveri and Narmada — have enhanced its spiritual growth as well. Each of these rivers is associated with a particular divine force.

The Ganga is associated with Shiva, Godavari with Rama, Yamuna with Krishna, Sindhu with Hanuman, Saraswati with Ganesha, Kaveri with Dattatreya and Narmada with Durga. India's culture developed and flourished mostly along the banks of these rivers upon which most of the ancient rishis and munis meditated, and unfolded divine and natural secrets. Of these rivers, the Ganga is the most important. The water of this river is so spiritually charged that if consumed with faith, it can redeem one from one's sins of several previous births.

The Ganga, in the strict sense of the word 'river', is not a natural river. A natural river is that which originates at some source or point and then follows its own course. In the case of the Ganga, the source is not natural but preconceived and determined by a human being—King Bhagirath of the Suryavamsa dynasty, and one of the forefathers of Rama.

According to legend, Bhagirath had undertaken severe penance to bring Ganga to earth from the heavens, to redeem the souls of his uncles by having it flow over their ashes. He had also searched for a source that was divine at its very roots. His father, King Dilip, and grandfather, King Sagar, had both been unsuccessful in their attempts to do so. After having identified the origin of the Ganga at Gomukh, in the Gangotri glacier in the Himalayas, Bhagirath charted Ganga's course, and thus purified the remains of his ancestors—the 60,000 sons of King Sagar—who had been reduced to ashes by Kapil Muni near the present-day Ganga Sagar, in the Bay of Bengal. It is evident from this legend that the chief objective of bringing down the Ganga to the plains was purely religious and spiritual, apart from the river serving as a great source for the socio-economic growth of India. While charting the course of the Ganga, Bhagirath ensured that it passed through certain other vital geo-locations such as Haridwar and Triveni so that on the occasion of the Kumbh—a mass pilgrimage in which Hindus gather at the banks of the river in Allahabad—a large number of people would receive spiritual strength. The holy locale of Gomukh is such that it receives specific radiations from heavenly bodies, particularly from the planet Jupiter.

In 1896, M.E. Hankin, a British bacteriologist who analysed the waters of all the major rivers of the world and that of Ganga concluded that the water of the Ganga was unique. It was the purest in addition to being a disinfectant. Later, a French doctor, Hairal, asserted that the waters of the Ganga were potent enough to destroy the germs of several diseases. In 1947, Kohiman, a water analyst from Germany, visited India and analysed a sample of water taken from the Ganga at Varanasi. He submitted a detailed report and affirmed that the waters of the river had a unique and great potency for killing germs and bacteria of many diseases. It is for these reasons that the Hindus immerse the ashes of their deceased into the Ganga, and believe that a dip into the holy waters will wash away their sins.

Apart from what modern scientists have found in the waters of the Ganga, our rishis and munis have always maintained that regular intake of the water helped them in attaining their spiritual sojourn. It is unfortunate that the present state of the Ganga is repelling. This great river is being polluted along its course from Haridwar onwards. There are reports that the Ganga is being polluted even at Gangotri. Every year, nearly a lakh of *kavariya*s (devotees of Shiva) reach Gangotri, putting immense pressure on the holy region. The government needs to take firm steps to check this menace if the divinity of the Ganga is to be maintained.

The natives of India are by nature vegetarians — *satvik* and non-voilent — which helps them to be less *tamasik* — aggressive and lethargic. Tolerance is the hallmark of Indian culture and it is for this reason that the endless hordes of invaders who came to India eventually settled down here and made it their home. No wonder that India is one of the oldest surviving cultures of the world, while many other contemporary ones have perished with time.

It may surprise many to know that there are as many as six seasons in a year in India. Most countries in the world have three to four seasons. With the coming of each new season, human chemistry changes too, bringing about certain variations in the human psyche and body. Rishis and munis have studied these transformations in man and have prescribed the consumption of specific seasonal fruits and vegetables while imposing restrictions on some. They advised people to observe a fast on particular days during the change of season, specifically on *amavasya*s or new moon nights, *purnima*s or full moon nights, and *ekadashi* or the eleventh day of each month. The human body releases certain bile juices on ekadashi, and if one allows these to be fully absorbed in the body, one is greatly benefited both physically and spiritually. It is for this reason that it is recommended that a fast be observed on this day. This speaks for the longevity of people in the past.

Certain plants and trees like the tulsi, neem and peepal have an important place in Hinduism. The tulsi plant is an integral part of a Hindu household. It has now been scientifically accepted that it is very sensitive to its surroundings. If there is any negativity in its immediate environs, it will wither away. Thus, it serves as a spiritual barometer of a household. Likewise, the neem tree too helps in warding off negativity from its vicinity. No wonder neem trees were grown around and within courtyards of houses in the old days. The peepal was an equally important tree and formed an inseparable part of old Hindu society. It is a perpetual source of oxygen, which, of course, is imperative for a healthy environment. Regularly sitting under a peepal tree invigorates the mind. For this reason, education was imparted under the shade of this tree in the old days. The air under the peepal carries great *pranik* (vital) value which is conducive to spiritual growth. The peepal and neem both are natural anti-pollutants.

In a nutshell, India's special geo-location on the planet, the two mountain ranges, i.e., the Aravallis and the Himalayas, the rivers with their spiritual sources of origin, the six seasons, and certain flora and fauna greatly attribute to its spiritual character. It is for these reasons that India has a divine aura around it and gave birth to four major religions of the world — Hinduism, Buddhism, Jainism and Sikhism.

GODS, GODDESSES AND NATURE

1

Why Is Lord Ganesha Worshipped First?

Literally, Ganesha means the king of *gana*s or earthly deities. He is also known as Vighneshwara or the dispeller of all obstacles.

Ganesha is regarded as the lord of the earth, just as Vishnu is the lord of Vaikuntha, the abode of Vishnu, and Shiva of Mount Kailash. According to legend, Ganesha was born from the peeled-off waste that his mother, Goddess Parvati, rubbed off from her body one day, before taking her bath. This goes to show that Ganesha is associated with the element of earth. For this reason, priests use a lump of earth in lieu of an image of Ganesha during certain rituals.

It is strongly believed that no human effort on earth is successful without the blessings of Lord Ganesha. Hence, he is propitiated before launching any new venture. Another reason to appease Ganesha first is that all human thoughts are expressed in the *naad-bhasha* or the language of words, but the language of gods, goddess and deities who live in the astral world is *prakash-bhasha* or the language of light. Ganesha is said to convert the naad-bhasha of human beings into the prakash-bhasha of the Divine so that human thoughts may reach the gods. Hence, he is worshipped first.

As the ruler of earth, Ganesha rules over the ten directions called *disha*. No divine power can descend on earth without his consent. Hence, for any divine force to bless human beings, Lord Ganesha is invoked to allow astral bodies to descend and bless people.

It is believed that when Lord Ganesha's idols are immersed after ten days of puja, he carries away with him all the misfortunes of his devotees.

Ganesha has two wives—Riddhi and Siddhi—and two sons—Shubha and Labha. People often write his sons' names on their accounts books and their coffers.

2

Why Is Lord Ganesha Offered Red Flowers and Blades of Grass?

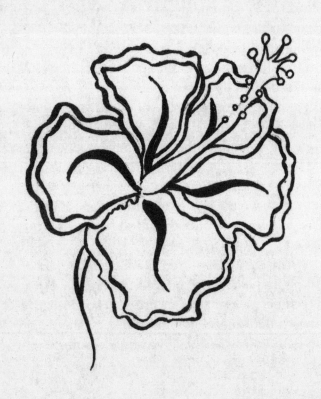

The *Shilpa Shastra*, the shastra that lays down the principles of architecture, states that the colour of Lord Ganesha is red. There are seven energy centres in a human body called the *sat chakras*, and each chakra has a specific colour. The first energy centre is the *muladhara* or the root chakra, the energy centre at the base of the spine, and its colour is red. Lord Ganesha is the presiding deity of this centre, and therefore, the colour red is consonant with him. It is because of this reason that red flowers are offered to him as they are in harmony with the vibrations of Lord Ganesha. Together with red flowers, red cloth and red sandalwood paste are also offered to him.

Another offering that finds favour with Lord Ganesha are tender grass blades called *drubh* or *durva*. These are offered in uneven numbers — one or three or five or seven — or in the form of a grass blades' garland. Grass blades are offered to Ganesha as it is believed that they have the power to attract Ganesha *tatwa*. The deity accepts these at once and the devotee is instantly blessed.

When red flowers, red cloth, red sandalwood, or durva grass blades are offered to Lord Ganesha, these enliven his idol, picture, or image. Therefore, to please Ganesha and to seek his blessings, he should only be offered such articles that give him pleasure.

3

Which God Is to Be Offered
Which Flower?

Gods and goddesses are divine beings and since they reside in the astral world, these divine bodies have the air element predominant in them. Subsequently, they have a keen sense of smell as, by their very nature, these heavenly beings love good smell and are naturally attracted to it, wherever it exists.

During various rituals, gods and goddesses are invoked to descend on earth from their respective abode by offering them objects of their choice. When they descend on this planet, they naturally gravitate towards the pleasing smell of flowers, perfumes and other articles that emit good fragrances. It is on account of their fondness for an amiable smell of flowers and incense that we use them during rituals.

Like human beings, gods and goddesses, too, have their preferences for a particular odour, scent, colour and flower. While some prefer the smell of the yellow marigold, others may prefer that of the white jasmine. Therefore, only such articles, objects, leaves and flowers are used in pujas and rituals that find favour with the presiding deity of the puja or ritual.

In Hinduism's holy scriptures, even the count or the number of flowers and special leaves that are to be offered is specified. Certain gods are to be offered three red flowers while some others may be presented five or nine of yellow or white flowers, together with the leaves of a particular tree.

When praying to Lord Vishnu, the offering of tulsi leaves is mandatory, while for Lord Shiva, it has to be bel leaves. Lord Ganesha is pleased by blades of the durva grass. Generally, gods and goddesses are to be offered five leaves or flowers, the number representing the five basic elements of nature—the panchabhootas. However, in certain specified tantric pujas, the number may vary.

The science behind offering flowers, leaves, scents and other aromatic substances is that they all have the characteristic of attracting positive and divine vibrations from the surroundings and thus sanctifying the puja area, charging the atmosphere with heavenly vibes. Mango leaves, in particular, have this quality of gathering divine vibes from the surrounding atmosphere. It is for this reason that a bunting of mango leaves called *toran* is tied over the puja area. For the same reason, nine or eleven mango leaves are put around the coconut that is placed at the mouth of a *kalash* or pot normally used for puja and similar rituals.

Fresh flowers and their petals have a limited life, beyond which they do not serve the purpose of attracting divine vibrations to charge up the ritual area. Once they have withered, they cannot be used for a puja. Some flowers and leaves stay fresh for a longer period of time. The lotus flower, tulsi and bel leaves, the amla fruit and lemon have a longer lifespan. They can retain their freshness for about three days and beyond due to the presence of *prana* and *dhananjaya vayu*s (prana is the most vital part of air that sustains life and dhananjaya maintains freshness). Tulsi and bel leaves can be re-used for puja after washing them.

A table showing the preferences of individual gods is given below.

Sr. No.	Gods and Goddesses	Name and Number of Flowers	Name and Number of Leaves or Fruit	Name of Scent
1	Ganesha	Any red flower	Durva grass blades: 1, 3, 5, 7 (Do not ever offer tulsi leaves to Ganesha)	Henna
2	Shiva	Blue lotus, any white flower, kaner (Do not offer champa and kewra flowers to Shiva)	Bel leaves: 9 or 10; also dhatura and aak	Kewra
3	Durga	Mogra	Bel leaves: 1 or 9	Mogra

Sr. No.	Gods and Goddesses	Name and Number of Flowers	Name and Number of Leaves or Fruit	Name of Scent
4	Mahakali	Yellow kaner: 9		
5	Vishnu	Pink lotus	Tulsi leaves: 1, 3, 5, 7, 9	Chandan
6	Lakshmi	Pink lotus: 9; yellow gaindha (marigold), desi gulab (not hybrid)	Shriphal (bel fruit): 1	Chandan
7	Rama	Chameli: 4		Chameli
8	Hanuman	Chameli	A garland made up of tulsi or aak leaves	Chameli
9	Krishna	Blue lotus: 3		Chandan
10	Dattatreya	Juhi: 7		Khas

Sr. No.	Gods and Goddesses	Name and Number of Flowers	Name and Number of Leaves or Fruit	Name of Scent
11	Brahma	Tagar and white lotus: 6		
12	Saraswati	Any white flower or white lotus: 9		

4

Which Image or Idol of Lord Ganesha Should Be Installed in Homes?

While buying an idol or a picture of Ganesha, always bear in mind that only such idols or pictures may be bought and brought home in which the Lord's trunk has been drawn or carved as turning to your right when you look at it. In other words, Ganesha's trunk should be turning to his own left side. Such images are auspicious for homes as they attract and generate positive energy. Images or idols in which the trunk turns towards the left side of Ganesha are called *vamamukhi murti*s. They bring in peace and prosperity because in these images, Ganesha's *chandra shakti* or lunar energy is active, and this is conducive for the material and spiritual growth of humans.

There are two types of energies that emanate from Ganesha—lunar and solar. The former flows from Ganesha's left nostril and is benign and beneficial to humans. On the contrary, the solar energy that flows from his right nostril is too powerful and cannot be borne by ordinary mortals and households. Therefore, the *dakshinamukhi murti*, as opposed to the vamamukhi murti is installed in temples, as Ganesha's solar energy is assimilated through regular pujas, rituals and observations, which are normally not possible in households.

The dakshinamukhi murtis represent the direction of Yamaloka (the abode of the Lord of death, Yamaraj) and hence attract negative energy which can disturb the peace of a home. However, such results are possible only when the idol is carved out or painted following the traditional tenets of the Shilpa Shastra. The idols and pictures of modern times do not have similar effects; nonetheless, one can follow the thumb rule about the trunk when choosing Ganesha's image or idol.

5

Why Do Hindus Half–Circumambulate a Shiva *Lingam*?

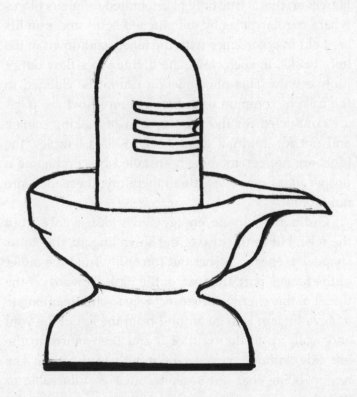

Generally, we complete a *pradakshina* or circumambulation around an idol in a temple, but in the case of the Shiva lingam, we go around only half the distance and do not complete the circle. The reason for not doing so is purely scientific.

The purpose of circumambulation is to receive divine vibrations that flow out of the deity's image and enter into our body to benefit us as we go around it. However, this is true only of celebrated religious places where regular pujas by enlightened souls and pundits are held in accordance with the tenets laid down in the holy books. In such cases, the divine vibes flow out of idols evenly. This phenomenon cannot be claimed in the case of common or roadside temples where pujas are conducted for the primary aim of making money and not for spiritual gain. Also, in such temples, the idols are not ceremoniously installed by conducting a proper *prana pratishtha* ritual; therefore, these idols are not vibrant.

Ordinarily, divine energy flows out evenly from the relic, but in the case of the Shiva lingam, due to its shape, the energy gushes out forcefully from the outlet of the female part, the *yoni*, of the idol. To ward off the thrust of this energy, the correct way to circumambulate a Shiva lingam is to go around from the left of the yoni and walk up to the right of it and then return to the left side without crossing the mouth of the yoni. The reason being that one's genital area is vulnerable to the channelized flow of the energy emanating out of that part of the image. There are several types of

18

*vayu*s or winds in a human body, of which *devadatta* and dhananjaya are two winds that are related to our reproductive system. The exposure of one's genital to that force of energy can harm the person crossing the mouth of the yoni, in particular, of male devotees.

6

What Is the Significance of
Panchamukhi Hanuman?

Hanuman is the incarnation of the tenth *rudra* or part of Lord Shiva, who is said to have eleven rudras in all. He was born to Kesari, the king of monkeys, and Anjana. As the son of Anjana, Hanuman is also known as Anjaneya. He is god incarnate of might and mind.

During the Rama–Ravana Lanka *yudh* or war, Hanuman assumed his panchamukhi or five-faced form to kill Ahiravana, a powerful demon, a black magician, and possessor of a mysterious weapon, the *nagapasha*, darts that would secretly inject serpent poison into human body. Ahiravana, the brother of Ravana, had taken Rama and Lakshmana to the netherworld as captives while the two were sleeping at night.

The only way to kill Ahiravana was to extinguish the five lamps lit up in five different directions, all at the same instant. To accomplish this almost impossible task, Hanuman assumed a panchamukhi form and blew out the lamps in one go. Rakshasa Ahiravana was killed and thus, Hanuman freed Rama and Lakshmana.

The five faces of Hanuman are that of an eagle, Garuda, facing the west; a boar, Varaha, facing the north; a horse, Hayagriva, facing the sky; a lion, Narasimha, facing the south; and the fifth being the original Hanuman, facing the east. The panchamukhi Hanuman has ten arms holding ten different weapons, including his own celebrated weapon, the *gada*.

This form of Hanuman is worshipped both in south India as well as in north India for protection from a variety of afflictions. The face towards the east is Hanuman's original form, the *kapimukha* or monkey face, whose worship removes all blemishes of one's past deeds and confers purity of mind. Devotion to this face appeases saturn too, and provides protection against its affliction.

The west-facing *garudamukha* drives away evil spells, black magic influences and negative spirits, and also flushes out all poisonous effects from the human body. It protects one from troubles and miseries brought about by one's spouse.

The north-facing *varahamukha* wards off ill effects caused by the negative influences of planets adversely placed in one's birth chart and confers all eight types of prosperity — *ashta aishwarya*s. This mukha also provides relief from sufferings created by the planet *Rahu*.

The south-facing *narashimhamukha* dispels fear of enemies and bestows victory over every opposition. Besides, it mitigates sufferings caused by the bad effects of Mars, the *mangaladosha*.

The sky-facing Hayagriva or *urdhvamukha* confers knowledge, victory, a good spouse, and also saves one from the curse of being childless.

One of the most famous pilgrimage centres — the Hanuman Dhara Temple, at Chitrakut, in central India — is said to be the resting place of Lord Hanuman. It is believed that after the coronation of Lord Rama, Hanuman requested him for a place where the burn injuries on his tail could be cured, which he incurred during the Lanka yudh. Rama then shot an arrow into the ground, and a stream of water spurted out from that spot. Rama asked Hanuman to rest there and cool the burning sensation in his tail with the waters. A 40-foot-tall monolithic green granite idol—green stands for wisdom—of panchamukhi Hanuman has been installed in Thiruvallur, in Tamil Nadu, which was known as Rudravarnam in olden days.

Hanuman was Surya's disciple. He had a great command over Sanskrit and his pronunciation was flawless. He is considered as the epitome of wisdom. Generally, it is believed that Hanuman remained a bachelor. However, some devotees in south India believe that Hanuman married Survachala, the daughter of his guru, Surya. This belief, however, is not acknowledged by most devotees. Interestingly, he had a son—not from Survachala—named Makaradhvaja, who fought alongside him when he went to Patalaloka or the netherworld to free Rama and Lakshmana from Ahiravana. After killing the demon Ahiravana, Hanuman coronated Makaradhvaja as the king of Patalaloka.

7

Why Is *Jal* (Water) Offered to Surya—the Sun God?

Our body has a great need for colours, as these are vital for the well-being of the different parts of our body system. It may surprise many to know that several parts of the human body have different colours. Our nerves are blue, the heart is red, kidneys and pancreas are brownish, the bones are white, and the brain nerves are in rainbow colours.

The rays of the sun are white, but when passed through a medium, they get broken into their basic hues. When we offer water or jal in the morning to the rising sun in the prescribed manner, the sheet of water falling on to the ground works as a medium to split the sun's rays into a spectrum of colours and enters our body to benefit us.

If you wish to offer water to the sun, you must do it in the correct and prescribed manner. Stand facing the sun with a vessel full of water. Hold the vessel at a level between the sun and your eyes. Then pour out the water slowly to the ground, allowing the sun's rays to pass through the sheet of water falling on the ground. The rays of the sun, while passing through the offered water, will break into their basic colours and fall on the face and thus enter the body of the person offering the water to benefit him spiritually as well as physically. However, some people hold the view that the water vessel should be held at chest level.

Receiving solar energy in this manner taps a natural source of Mother Nature for our benefit, with no side effects. Hindu scriptures state that the ultraviolet rays of the sun destroy the bacteria of several deadly diseases. Therefore, while offering water, a mantra is uttered:

Om Rogiam Vinashaya Dev Jyoti Namaste

Besides curing and warding off diseases, one improves ones eyesight too by worshipping the sun god, surya. Astrologically, the sun is symbolic of one's eyes, soul and father. Therefore, offering water to surya mitigates past life karma, ill deeds done against one's father, enhances eyesight and elevates one spiritually.

8

Why Is the River Ganga Sacred?

The *Shiva Purana* states that during the *Treta Yuga*, the second leg of the Hindu Age, the Puranic king Bhagirath prayed to Lord Brahma and Lord Shiva to allow the Ganga to descend to earth to redeem his ancestors. Hindus earnestly believe that bathing in the waters of the Ganga redeems one's sins. It is also believed that when the ashes of a person are immersed in the Ganga, they soon dissolve in the jala tatwa. Even modern scientists have accepted that bottled Gangajal remains bacteria-free for months together.

What is so special about the Ganga that makes it different from other rivers of the country? There are many important rivers in India, like the Yamuna, Godavari, Krishna, Kaveri, Sindhu and Brahmaputra. Each of these rivers has a natural source and has carved out its own course or path—except the Ganga—which is the only river whose source was pre-decided and developed by man and not by nature. Further, its course too was chartered by man and not by nature. It was King Bhagirath who discovered the source of the Ganga and later chartered its course along certain significantly located cities such as Haridwar, Varanasi, Allahabad and Patna. In the light of these facts, the Ganga cannot be called a natural river—it is much more than that.

According to legend, King Bhagirath's grandfather and father, King Sagar and King Dilip, respectively, started searching for a waterbody that was divine at its source, but in vain. Finally, Bhagirath reached the exact location of the desired waterbody in its frozen state, at Gomukh, in the Gangotri glacier. Here, Bhagirath observed that, thanks to the heavenly radiations from the planet Jupiter, the entire expanse of this frozen block had turned into divine water. In fact, Gomukh is a unique and rare geo-point on earth that receives special rays from Jupiter as it is located at the intersection of a distinct longitude and latitude of the globe. The entire stretch of the frozen area measured nearly 24 sq km and was 300 ft deep. However, due to global warming, this area has now reduced in size. This phenomenon does not occur anywhere else in the world and because of this extraordinary factor, the Ganga is the only river whose waters can redeem one of sins.

Additionally, the glacier receives moonbeams — Shiva tatwa — at night, which aids in freezing the water and during the day, it is under the melting rays of the sun — Vishnu tatwa. The process continues unabated day and night, impacting the quality of the water. However, the principal reason behind the divine quality of Gangajal is due to Jupiter. Thus, Ganga's water is unique, divine, and stays bacteria-free for several months. Moreover, there are some physical factors too that are described later in the book.

It is unfortunate that the present state of the Ganga and its waters is so very dismal. Factories in the cities located on its banks pollute the waters with their poisonous discharge that has made it unworthy for human consumption. Its divinity and the past glory all seem to have disappeared due to human intervention. In a serious bid to restore its lost glory, the Government of India has declared the Ganga as the national river, and has devised the Ganga Action Plan to clean its waters.

Why Does Bottled Gangajal Remain Bacteria-Free?

Hindus regard the Ganga as a redeemer of sins, and hence many Hindu pilgrimage sites are located on the banks of this river. Its water is considered next to nectar and is administered even to a dying man.

Scientifically, the Ganga's waters have certain unique properties that are found in the waters of no other river of the country — maybe even of the world. According to an environmental engineering study conducted by the University of Roorkee, Uttarakhand, the Ganga has a remarkable capacity for self-purification. This amazing characteristic is attributed to the fact that at the very source at Gangotri, its water receives certain divine radiations from the sun, moon and Jupiter, making her water as exceptional as nectar and redeemer of sins.

The ability to destroy bacteria is a quality that probably no other river of the world can claim. In 1947, a German scientist, Kohiman, came to India and took a sample of the Ganga water from Varanasi and conducted experiments. He later authored a paper on his findings, where he mentioned that, 'The Ganga-waters have a stunning quality of destroying bacteria which I haven't observed in the water of other rivers of the world.' The French scientist, Havel, also made a similar observation on Gangajal. He asserted that this water can destroy the germs of many diseases. Therefore, a man who regularly consumes Gangajal will remain disease-free. The findings of the University of Roorkee confirmed that the water of the Ganga is a disinfectant, self-purifying and can kill bacteria that cause cholera.

Since Gangajal is a disinfectant, it is sprinkled over places, on people, and on objects while performing a puja. The act of sprinkling Gangajal is called *shudhikaran*. In modern parlance, it means disinfecting the place, people and objects prior to starting a ritual. Hindus administer Gangajal to a dying man to mitigate his suffering.

Interestingly, the Rig Veda maintains that the now non-existent river Saraswati was older than the Ganga — as is river Narmada as well. In fact, the name of Ganga is very rarely mentioned in the scriptures, whereas the names of Saraswati and Narmada are liberally mentioned in the Vedas; yet Ganga is the sacred-most river and a redeemer of sins.

9

Why Do Hindus Venerate Mother Nature?

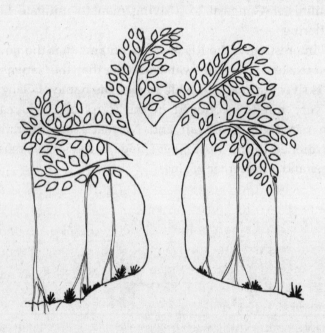

Human life on earth depends on plants and trees. They provide us with everything that makes life possible on earth: oxygen, food, rainfall, shelter, clothing, medicines, and so on. Hence, the Vedic man had deep love and respect for Mother Nature, and a sense of ecological responsibility. He considered *prithvi* or earth as a *devi* or goddess. The hymn to the earth, in *Bhumi Sukta*, a beautiful ode to Mother Earth containing sixty-three verses, clearly reveals the Vedic man's rapport with, reverence for, and propitiation of the powers latent in Mother Nature.

Nature or *vanaspati* is regarded as a benevolent mother, and is therefore revered by Hindus. Most Vedic hymns are about gods of nature whom the Aryans worshipped. The rishis and munis studied vanaspati in depth and devised ways to be in harmony with the elements of nature. The concept of conducting *yagna*s was primarily aimed at purifying the surrounding atmosphere. The firewood, herbs, plants, dry fruits and ghee, used in yagnas, were such that they had a non-polluting effect when burnt, and instead, sanitized the environment. These are scientific facts, not myths.

In the past, every village had several peepal, banyan, neem and other trees that purified the atmosphere. Temple compounds had *sthala vriksha* — a special tree within the precincts of the temple compound, for performing puja. The tulsi was an essential part of every household in India in ancient times. Many families still nurse the tulsi plant in their homes. It is believed that divine beings manifest as trees and plants. The peepal tree is worshipped throughout the year whereas the banyan tree or *vata* has its day on *savitri vrata* purnima, in the month of *jyaishtha* or May–June.

In fact, in ancient times, preservation of vanaspati was part of the Hindu way of thinking. The Hindu thought is eco-friendly and aims at maintaining a balance between man and nature. Vedic man looked upon the natural environment as a world of spiritual reality. The earth and its creatures, including trees, forests, rivers and oceans, rocks and mountains, and the world beyond—the stars and the skies—all appeared to him as powerful and resonating with the Supreme Spirit. He saw in them the same life that was in him.

Hindus believed that every tree, every plant, big or small, had a spirit, and therefore, felling a tree was considered an act of demerit. Indian scriptures tell us to plant ten trees on felling one. Had we followed this age-old practice, the present-day alarming eco-imbalance situation would not have arisen.

Amongst the Gonds of central India, prior to felling a tree, a man had to beg its pardon for the injury he would inflict on it. When a tree had to be felled in the olden days, people would pour ghee on the stump, saying: 'Grow thou out of this.'

*Vaidya*s or physicians would seek permission from medicinal plants/shrubs/trees before plucking their leaves or removing their bark. Since plants have life, their pardon for the injury inflicted on them necessitated such an act. This shows the depth of concern and care that Vedic society had towards vanaspati, the sustaining force of life on earth.

10

Why Is the Peepal Tree
Considered Sacred?

The peepal is considered the most sacred tree in India. Historical evidence proves that this tree grew even during the days of the Indus Valley Civilization (IVC). A seal found at Mohenjo-Daro, one of the cities of the IVC (3,000–1,700 BC) shows the peepal being worshipped. Testimonials indicate that during the Vedic times, the wood of the peepal was used to make fire by friction. The tree has enjoyed great eminence since the early days of Indian society and is regarded as the king of all trees.

In Hindu thought, the peepal is associated with the *Sanatan* trinity: Brahma, Vishnu and Mahesh/Shiva. According to popular belief, the tree houses the *trimurti* — its roots represent Brahma, the trunk Vishnu and the branches Shiva. The gods are said to hold their councils under the tree — hence the tree assumes ample spiritual significance. Another unique feature of this revered tree is that its roots creep upwards unlike the banyan tree whose roots fall from above to the ground, symbolizing that the peepal tree alleviates man from the mortal world to the immortal one.

The *Brahma Purana* and the *Padma Purana* — ancient texts in Sanskrit containing mythological accounts of ancient times — relate that Vishnu once hid in a peepal tree when the gods lost a battle against the demons. Therefore, spontaneous worship to Vishnu can be offered to a peepal tree without needing his image or temple. The *Skanda Purana* considers the peepal to be a symbol of Vishnu, who is said to have been born under this tree.

The peepal is also closely linked to Krishna. In the Bhagavad Gita, the Lord says: 'Among trees, I am the *ashwattha*'. Krishna is believed to have died under this tree, after which the present *Kali Yuga* – Man in this age is farthest from Mother Nature, His social and moral standards are at the lowest – is said to have begun.

During the Vedic days, the peepal tree was known as *ashwattha*. The great spiritual saint, Adi Shankaracharya, explains that the tree represents the entire cosmos. *Shwa* in Sanskrit means 'tomorrow', *a* indicates negation, and *tha* means 'one that remains'. He, therefore, interprets ashwattha to indicate 'one which does not remain the same tomorrow, like the ever-changing universe itself'. However, ashwattha literally means 'where horses are rested' or 'the resting place for horses'. In Sanskrit *ashwa* means 'horse' and *tha* means 'a place', hence the name, ashwattha. In ancient times, horses were the main means of transportation. The tree provided shelter to the animal under its sprawling, big branches and cooling shade.

The tree has several other names: *bo*-tree, *bodhi*, *pimpalla*, *pimpal*, *jari*, *arani*, *ragi*, *bodhidruma*, *shuchidruma*, *rukkha arayal* and *kaavam*. Its heart shaped leaves have long, tapering tips. The slightest breeze makes them rustle, giving it the name of *chanchala* or vibrant.

A large, fast-growing deciduous tree, the peepal is of medium size and has a large crown with wonderful, wide spreading branches. It sheds its leaves in the months of March and April. The fruits of the peepal are hidden within the figs. Although the peepal can be found all over the country, it is mainly seen in Haryana, Bihar, Kerala and Madhya Pradesh. It is the state tree of Haryana, Bihar and Orissa. The peepal is also found in the Ranthambore National Park in Rajasthan.

This ashwattha tree is quite remarkable because it grows both upwards as well as top to bottom. The branches themselves morph into roots, so even if the original tree decays and perishes, its underlying branches are young and continue to enclose the parent. This eternal life of the peepal tree has inspired both Indian philosophers and Hindu thought. It is not uncommon to run into an ashwattha tree that is a few hundred or even one thousand years old. The one at Bodhgaya as well as the one in Sri Lanka are two notable examples of such old trees. In fact, it is one of the longest-living trees in the world.

According to the *Skanda Purana*, if one does not have a son, the peepal should be regarded as one. As long as the tree lives, the family name will continue. To cut down a peepal is considered a sin equivalent to killing a Brahmin, one of the five deadly sins known as *panchapataka*. The *Skanda Purana* further states that for committing such a deed, the person will go to hell and all his good deeds will come to naught. However, cutting the branches of this tree for yagna or sacrificial fire, and offering its dried wood into the yagna fire are acts of great merit. Since the tree is considered sacred, people place their damaged idols, old calendars and pictures bearing figures of gods and goddesses at its base.

Parikrama or circumambulation of the holy peepal tree and pouring water on it daily destroys all kinds of inauspiciousness. Pouring water on the roots of this tree in the month of *vaishakha* (May–June) begets immense virtue, and worshipping it with devotion grants long life and prosperity.

Some people avoid going near or touching the peepal on all days other than Saturdays. The *Brahma Purana* explains why. Once upon a time, two demons, Ashwattha and Peepala, harassed people. Ashwattha would take the form of a peepal tree and Peepala the form of a Brahmin. The fake Brahmin would advise people to touch the tree, and as soon as they did, Ashwattha would kill them. Eventually, they were both killed by Shanidev. Therefore, it is considered safe to touch the tree on Saturdays. Moreover, since Goddess Lakshmi is also believed to inhabit the tree on Saturdays, it is considered auspicious to worship it on that day. Women who seek the birth of a son tie a red thread or red cloth around its trunk or on its branches.

As the peepal tree has medicinal qualities, it is used extensively in Ayurveda. The juice of its leaves, extracted by holding these near fire, can be used as an eardrop. A powder made from its bark heals wounds of yesteryears, while the bark itself is useful in treating inflammations and glandular swelling of the neck. Its root is useful for stomatitis, cures ulcers and promotes granulations. Its roots are also good for gout. The roots are even chewed to prevent gum diseases. Its fruit also offers a host of benefits: it works as a laxative, aiding digestion; checks vomiting; is good for foul taste, thirst and heart diseases; and taken in powdered form, it is beneficial for asthma. The seeds are useful in urinary troubles. Also, the leaves of the peepal are used to treat constipation.

The tree has some other uses as well. Its bark yields a reddish dye. Its leaves are used to feed camels and elephants. Dried peepal leaves are used for decoration purposes.

The peepal is considered holy by Buddhists as well, since Gautama Buddha attained enlightenment under a peepal tree at Bodhgaya. Hence, it is also called the bodhi tree or the tree of enlightenment. Traditional Buddhist records indicate that a branch of the tree was carried to Sri Lanka in 288 BC by Emperor Ashoka's son and daughter, and was planted there. This tree can be seen even now. Buddhists, regard the tree as the personification of the Buddha. Emperor Ashoka also planted peepal trees on both sides of the roads in most parts of his empire. It is said that Ravana, the demon king of Lanka, who knew about the wonderful properties of the tree, got thousands of peepal trees planted in his kingdom.

But, if we examine the tree from the perspective of science and not that of religion or spiritualism, we find that even here, it scores high marks! It is believed that this is the only tree in the world that exhales oxygen all the twenty-four hours of the day (Source: *Vrikshayurveda*, a book authored by Surapala between the tenth and fourteenth centuries). The air that passes through the dancing leaves of the peepal destroys bacteria and germs present in the atmosphere; thus the peepal is a natural purifier. For this reason, in olden days, all villages had several peepal trees within their boundaries.

When you sit under a peepal tree, your brain cells get rejuvenated. For this reason, ancient ashrams had several peepal trees, beneath which gurus held lessons. Since the tree has environmental significance, Hindus accord it social sanctity. They also hold the view that the tree is the abode of certain astral bodies like ghosts and vampires because the environs of the tree are conducive for them.

Commensurate with Indian cultural heritage and keeping in mind the significance of the tree, India's highest civilian award, the Bharat Ratna, is awarded on a replica of a peepal tree, in bronze.

11

Why Is the Tulsi Plant
Considered Sacred?

Revered in India for over 5,000 years, the tulsi plant holds great importance in a traditional Hindu home. This plant is nurtured with care and reverence, and the ladies of an orthodox Hindu household worship it diligently. The tulsi plant is grown in the centre of the house, on an altar-like structure called tulsi *chaura*. Indians consider it as one of the most sacred plants.

Tulsi leaves are an essential ingredient of the *panchamrita* in a puja ceremony. In fact, it is known to be the only holy object which, once used in worship, can be cleaned and reused in yet another puja because it purifies itself.

A garland made solely of tulsi leaves is the first offering to the Lord during the daily *alankaran* ritual. It is believed that all offerings to Lord Vishnu are incomplete without the tulsi leaf—perhaps because the vibrations of a tulsi *mala* (garland) are said to be in harmony with Lord Vishnu's vibrations. In Vaishnava philosophy, tulsi leaves please Lord Vishnu the most. Rosaries—tulsi malas—are made from the dried stems of the plant. Vaishnavites always use tulsi mala, particularly while reciting Vishnu mantras.

According to folklore, once, Lord Krishna—one of the avatars of Vishnu—held a *tulabharam*, a religious practice of weighing a person against coins, grain, vegitables, gold, etc., in which he sat on one of the pans of the balance scale. On the other pan of the balance, all the gold ornaments of his queen, Satyabhama, were placed. Even then the weight of these ornaments could not outweigh Krishna! However, a single tulsi leaf—

placed on the other side by his second queen, Rukmini — tilted the balance. The anecdote goes to show that even Lord Krishna regarded tulsi as superior to himself.

The tulsi is the queen of all Indian herbs. Although none of the Puranas describe the tulsi as feminine, tulsi symbolizes Goddess Lakshmi, the consort of Lord Vishnu. Those who wish to be righteous and have a happy family life worship the tulsi. Along with other Hindu gods and goddesses, tulsi is worshipped in the Tulsi Manas Mandir at Varanasi.

Hindus perform a special tulsi puja annually on the ekadashi of *shukla paksha* or the eleventh bright day of the month of *kartika*. On this day, the tulsi is ceremonially married to Lord Vishnu. A tulsi plant, grown in an earthen pot, is decorated like a bride and Vishnu, in the form of a *shaligrama*, a black fossil found on the bed of the river Gandaki, in Nepal, is placed in the potted tulsi to symbolize the marriage. The ritual is called tulsi *vivaha*. The day the ritual is performed inaugurates the marriage season, especially in north India.

According to one legend, Tulsi was the devoted and pious wife of Shankhachuda, a celestial demon who had terrorized the gods. It was believed that the source of Shankhachuda's strength was his chaste and devoted wife. To weaken the demon's strength, Lord Vishnu tricked her into sinning. When she realized the trick, she cursed Lord Vishnu to turn into a black stone — shaligrama. Seeing her devotion and adherence to righteousness, Vishnu blessed her and said that she would continue to live on earth as a blessed plant —

worshipped and adorned on his head. Thereafter, the tradition of tulsi vivaha began. Vishnu also said that all offerings to him would be incomplete without the tulsi leaf. Interestingly, tulsi leaves are never offered to Lord Ganesha.

A Sanskrit *shloka* describes the tulsi as 'the incomparable one' in its qualities. Apart from its religious significance, the tulsi has great medicinal value too. Modern scientific research offers impressive evidence that the tulsi reduces stress, enhances stamina, relieves inflammation, lowers cholesterol, eliminates toxins, protects against radiation, prevents gastric ulcers, lowers fevers, improves digestion, and provides a rich supply of antioxidants and other nutrients. It is a rich antioxidant and is also known for its restorative qualities. Moreover, this unique plant is especially effective in supporting the heart, blood vessels, liver and lungs, and also regulates blood pressure and blood sugar.

An essential oil extracted from *karpoora* tulsi — a variety of tulsi — is mostly used for medicinal purposes, though, of late, it is used even in the manufacture of herbal toiletries. Recently, organic tulsi has also been developed for the first time as a stress reliever and energizer.

The tulsi is said to be a great mosquito repellent as well. In a letter written to *The Times*, London, dated 2 May 1903, Dr George Birdwood, Professor of Anatomy, Grant Medical College, Bombay, said: 'When the Victoria Gardens were established in Bombay, the men employed on those works were pestered by mosquitoes. At the recommendation of the Hindu managers, the whole boundary of the gardens was planted with holy basil, on which the plague of mosquitoes was at once abated, and fever altogether disappeared from among the resident gardeners.'

Yet another property of the tusli leaves is that they can absorb ultraviolet radiation, which is why tulsi leaves are placed on food items during an eclipse — to protect them from radiation.

A few things have to be kept in mind when tending to the tulsi plant. It is very sensitive to any strong odour. Therefore, if a lady touches the plant during her menstrual cycle or even goes near it, the plant will soon wither away. Then again, the plant discharges electrical impulses at night which are harmful to humans, and so it is forbidden to pluck tulsi leaves at night. For this reason, the tulsi is also known as *vrinda*, which means electric energy. Further, tulsi leaves have a certain quantity of mercury which is harmful for the gums. Therefore, tulsi leaves have to be swallowed when given as *prasad* and are not to be chewed.

There are two varieties of tulsi — Krishna tulsi or *Ocimum sanctum* and Rama or Vana tulsi or *Ocimum gratissimum*. The black-leaf tulsi is known as Krishna or Shyama tulsi and has different properties. The Rama tulsi or the Karpoora tulsi is commonly used for worship. Yet another variety of the tulsi is known as 'holy basil' in English, and is used as a flavouring ingredient in recipes.

Necklaces made of small tulsi beads are worn by the pious. Wearing a tulsi mala develops a magnetic field around a person and also checks dissipation of his static energy. The manufacture of a tulsi mala is a cottage industry in most pilgrim towns of India, especially Mathura and Vrindavan in Uttar Pradesh.

Among Hindus, water soaked with tulsi leaves is given to the dying to raise his departing soul to heaven. In Malaysia, tulsi is planted and worshipped in graveyards; similar beliefs are prevalent in Israel as well.

12

Why Is the Lotus Considered Sacred in Hindu Tradition?

The lotus represents the essence of Indian philosophy in a striking, symbolic way. It is the most beautiful icon that presents India's culture and thought to the world. Gods and goddesses in the Hindu pantheon hold the lotus in their hand or use it as their divine seat. It stands for truth, auspiciousness and beauty — *satyam, shivam, sundaram*. The Supreme Lord also has the same attributes and, therefore, his various parts are compared to a lotus — lotus-eyes, lotus-feet, lotus-hands, and the lotus of the heart.

According to the *Vishnu Purana*, a lotus emerged from the navel of Lord Vishnu, out of which appeared Lord Brahma to create the world. The lotus thus serves as the link between the Creator and the Supreme Cause. It also signifies Brahmaloka, the abode of Lord Brahma.

The flower is found in three colours: white, pink and blue. White lotus is known *pundarik*, and is offered to Brahma; pink lotus is called *kokanad*, and is associated with Vishnu; while the blue lotus is known as *indivar*, and is associated with Shiva. White lotus is seen held by Goddess Saraswati, pink by Mahalakshmi, and blue lotus by Parvati.

This divine flower is known by many names: *kamal, ambuj, neeraj, padma, arvind, saroj, pushkar, kumud, mrinalini, pankaj* and *utpal*. Another name for the lotus is *naal*, after which the ancient Buddhist university was named Nalanda — 'that which confers knowledge'.

The lotus symbolizes divinity, fertility, wealth, knowledge and enlightenment. The auspicious sign of the Swastika is also said to have evolved from the lotus.

It blooms with the rising sun and closes with sunset, following the course of the sun. It, therefore, stands for the highest and the purest of spiritual conceptions. Its close relation with water makes it the symbol of universal life.

Despite growing in slushy areas and in murky water, the lotus remains beautiful and untainted. It inspires us to strive to remain pure and noble in all our thoughts and actions under all circumstances. The lotus leaf never gets wet even though it constantly remains in water, symbolizing the man of wisdom, who doesn't get swayed by sorrow or joy. Just as the lotus leaf remains unpolluted by the water on which it floats, so too remains the man untainted and detached who dedicates all his actions to the lotus-feet of the Brahman or the Supreme Being.

The human body has certain energy centres that have been described in the yoga scriptures as *chakra*s. Each centre is associated with a lotus that has a certain number of petals. For example, the energy centre in the form of a lotus flower at the top of one's head has a thousand petals; it is called the *sahasra* chakra or the crown chakra. This chakra opens up when a yogi attains godhood or self-realization. The *padmasana* or the lotus posture is recommended when one sits for meditation. Moreover, the temple architecture of India and the ancient Indian village and town planning systems have been greatly influenced by the 'lotus concept'. In the past, the king or the central figure and the subjects under him where so placed that they spread out in a circular way from the centre, depending upon their vocations. Thus, the lotus has played, and continues to play, an important role in the everyday life of India. It is this continued significance and philosophical importance attached to the flower that makes it the national flower of India.

The symbolism of the lotus spread from India to Egypt via Persia (modern Iran), and from there to the Western world. In Buddhism, the lotus stands for the miraculous birth of Prince Siddhartha or the Buddha. Buddhists popularized the lotus in Tibet, China, Japan, Indonesia, and other island states in the Indian Ocean. In Jainism too, the symbolism of lotus does not differ much from that of Buddhism and Hinduism.

IMPORTANT HINDU
DATES

Significant Days and Dates in the Indian Tradition

The Indian calendar has a long list of festivals which vary in their origin. While some are celebrated as the birthdays of gods, saints or national heroes, others are held on occurrence of change of seasons or the origin of myths and legends of the land.

Peculiarly, there is yet another reason for festivals to be celebrated: on account of astronomical and astrological occurrences.

Makar sankranti, that falls every year around 14 January, is a date that has astronomical as well as scientific and medical significance. This is the day when the sun transits from the *dhanu rashi* or Sagittarius to *makar rashi* or Capricorn. It is on this date that the sun moves up from the southern sphere to the northern sphere, as a result of which the days become longer and the severity of the winter becomes milder. This change of position of the sun has a spiritual significance too. From this day onwards, the flight of human souls of pious people who die after this day onwards can easily soar higher into the upper regions of the cosmos. It is so because the air, due to increased intensity of heat, becomes lighter and the soul sails upwards with less resistance. Bhishma Pitamaha of the Mahabharata fame, though he fell on the battlefield on the tenth day of the battle in the month of November, breathed his last at his will after fifty-eight days when the sun had moved to a particular position in the northern sphere from the southern sphere.

The West has yet to study this aspect of human life. However, Indian scientists of yesteryears, the wise rishis and munis, had carried out vast research in the field of metaphysics and spiritualism and matter related to life after death; hence the conclusion about the faster ascent of the soul after makar sankranti.

Owing to the severe cold during winter, particularly in the north of the country, the temperature of the human body tends to be low. Therefore, toxic matters get accumulated, which are obviously harmful. A simple, practical, yet scientific method to flush out the toxins from the human system at the end of the winter is to consume *til* or sesame seed laddus and *rewari*s or sweatmeats for forty days, beginning makar sankranti until Holi. Medically, sesame seeds have natural characteristics to absorb and flush out toxins.

In the month of February, as the earth traverses further along the sun's orbit, comes the festival of Vasant Panchami, now known as Basant Panchami. In terms of comparative cultural significance, the festival can be compared to the Chinese New Year and the Christian Candlemass. On this fifth day of the month of *magha*, traditionally, yellow clothes are worn, and sweet saffron rice cooked, especially in north India, to herald the onset of vasant or spring. This day is considered very auspicious for initiating young ones into education. In olden days young pupils were led to temples or under the shade of peepel trees for initiating them into education after having performed the Saraswati Puja.

Though times have changed now and we follow the British calendar to admit children into schools in the months of April–May, Basant Panchami is still celebrated as is Saraswati Puja which is still performed on this day. Till around the 1950s, men and women used to be seen zealously flying kites on this day. Mustard fields are resplendent with their tiny yellow flowers in full bloom, ready for harvesting. Varieties of flowers start blooming around this time, and there is a sweet fragrance in the air.

In the ancient times, owing to the beauty of nature all around, Basant Panchami was oriented more towards Kamadev, the god of love. It is believed that on this day, Kamadev had trounced Lord Shiva by disturbing him from his deep yogic trance at the behest of other gods so as to persuade him to marry Parvati, the daughter of Himavat, the king of the northern Himalayas. Thus, Basant Panchami is associated with Kamadev, his wife, Rati, and their friend Vasant (the personification of the season of spring).

A special festival called Vasantmahotsav used to be celebrated on the day of Basant Panchami. In other parts of the country, it was celebrated as Dadhi Kamdho.

Even though times have changed, people are still seen wearing yellow clothes and cooking sweet saffron yellow rice to keep the tradition alive today.

13
Significance of Makar Sankranti

Indian sages and seers made detailed studies of the movement of planets in relation to the sun and the earth. There are twelve zodiac signs that are constantly in motion. Therefore, the position of the sun varies from time to time in relation to a particular zodiac. According to the Indian astrological system, the transition of the sun from one zodiac to another is called sankranti. Since there are twelve zodiacs, there are twelve sankrantis, of which makar sankranti is of great importance. During this sankranti, which falls around 14 January every year, the sun transits from the southern sphere to the northern sphere by moving from Sagittarius or dhanu rashi to Capricorn or makar rashi—Hence the name makar sankranti. The actual time of the transition is fleeting and cannot normally be viewed with naked eyes. However, there is a place, the famous Sabarimala shrine in Kerala, from where the auspicious transition of the sun can be seen even with naked eyes for a few seconds. The exact duration of the movement of the sun's transition is known as makar *jyoti*.

Similarly, when the sun moves from the northern hemisphere to the southern hemisphere around mid-July, the transition is known as *karkat* sankranti. This day onwards, the sun moves away from the earth, resulting in shorter days and causing winter in the region around the Indian subcontinent. Shorter days and softer intensity of the sun's rays change the inner chemistry of both human beings and nature. The period between these two sankrantis—karkat to makar—is known as *dakshinayan*. The sun remains below the equator towards the South Pole in this period.

On the auspicious day of makar sankaranti, people observe a fast and worship the sun. In the evening, they eat sesame seeds or til in the form of laddus and rewaris or other similar sweetmeats. Linseed has the power to absorb inner negativities caused by the effect of winter. After makar sankranti, the temperature on earth starts to gradually warm up and once again transforms the inner human chemistry and that of the trees and plants on earth. Makar sankranti, therefore, is an important event in the Hindu calendar that denotes planetary transition as well as change in human chemistry.

Holi: A Science and an Astrological Event beyond Colours

Holi is an ancient festival that dates back to the Vedic era of Indian history. After makar sankranti, as the earth advances along the sun's orbit and the *phalguna* purnima or full moon occurs, it marks the end of winter and the onset of the spring season. After this purnima commences the Hindu calendar with its first month: *chaitra*. It starts when the moon completely turns full. It is an astronomical event when the winter bids goodbye and the summer sets in. In fact, Holi is celebrated at the approach of vernal equinox. Originally, during the Vedic age, Holi was not celebrated the way it is today. Fun and frolic were added to the festivity later in the history of the land. In fact, the spirit of the original Holi festival was in the ritual of cleansing and purifying the atmosphere to ward off the impending danger of falling sick due to change of season.

Vedic people, therefore, thought of a ritual which was a remedy for the danger ahead. It was a two-day celebration wherein the rituals adopted by the Vedic men were scientific, eco-friendly, and socially sound.

The playful throwing of natural coloured powders on each other had a medical significance. The basic powder would come from tapioca and sago. The colours were traditionally made of neem and *bilva* leaves, kumkum and haldi, and with the flowers of *palash*, also called *taysu* or the flame of the forest, *aparajita* and marigold. Powdered and fragrant red sandalwood, dried hibiscus flowers, and pomegranate were alternative source of different shades of red. Mixing lime with turmeric created an alternative source of orange. The powder was sometimes combined with mica powder to create a twinkling effect.

Unfortunately, chemically produced industrial dyes and fake *abir* and *gulal* powders have replaced the natural colours. Medical reports confirm the harmful effects of such colours on the human body.

Another scientific reason for celebrating Holi is the tradition of Holika Dahan. When the Holika or bonfire is torched, its temperature rises to about 145°F, destroying the bacteria present in the atmosphere. Following the Vedic tradition, people are supposed to perform three or seven parikramas or circumambulations around the Holi bonfire; this kills the bacteria in the body.

In Holika bonfire, earlier only cow dung and timber of certain eco-friendly trees — *arrad*, *redi*, mango and palash — were used. The bonfire was ignited not by matchsticks but by reciting mantras at the exact mahurat when the moon completely turned full, to announce the commencement of chaitra month of the Hindu calendar. Since Holi also marked the beginning of the rabi agricultural season, freshly harvested grains, dry fruits and withered leaves were used as *ahuti* or offerings into the Holika bonfire. The smoke of the cow dung emitting from the bonfire was not only non-poisonous and eco-friendly, it also killed the bacteria in the air, owing to the high phosphorus content in it.

The festival of Holi has cultural and social significance too. It is a festival to end and rid oneself of past errors and mutual conflicts by meeting, greeting and embracing others. Thus, Holi is a festival of friendship and forgiveness, meant to create harmony in the society while simultaneously flushing out stagnant winter negativity.

Immediately, after three full days past after Holi, a minor but very significant day, known as *basauda*, meaning stale food, is observed, particularly in north India. The significance is that after this day, it was prohibited to consume stale food. It was calculated that bacterial germination in cooked food would start taking place with effect from the day of basauda, owing to weather conditions (obviously, no refrigerators were there when this tradition was introduced). The lady of the house would cook festive food on the eve of basauda, and the entire family would consume the same food the next day. Thereafter, stale food was not to be consumed until the onset of the next winter. Such old and significant traditions show that the ancient Indian rituals are not mere dogmas, but are based on pure scientific reasoning.

14

Significance of *Akshaya Tritiya*

According to the Hindu theory of creation, *kaal* or time) is a manifestation of God. The past, present and future all coexist in Him simultaneously. Therefore, God as *kaalpurush* is timeless and beyond its realms. According to Hindu thought, creation begins when God activates both His positive and negative energies; and it ends as He withdraws them into a state of inaction. Another important aspect of the Sanatan dharma theory of time is that time moves in a cyclical manner, commonly referred to as *kaalchakra*. The end of one cycle is the beginning of another—therefore, there is actually no end to creation. In a particular cycle of time, there are some timespans when God's positive energies are hyperactive. Such periods, when nature's positive energies are supercharged are known as mahurats or auspicious timings. Traditional Hindus believe in this theory of auspicious timing and follow it in every station and walk of life—be it to begin a new venture or making an important purchase.

Akshaya tritiya is one such momentous occasion. This *tithi* or date is considered one of the most auspicious days of the Hindu calendar. Akshaya tritiya is also known as *akhateej*. In Sanskrit, the word *akshaya* means imperishable or eternal or that which never diminishes. Akshaya tritiya is a holy day in the Jain calendar as well.

Ventures launched or valuables bought on this day are considered to bring success or unending good fortune. Associated with material gains and wealth acquisition, buying gold is a popular activity on akshaya tritiya, as it is the ultimate symbol of wealth and prosperity. Gold bought and worn on this day signifies never-diminishing good fortune. Hindus celebrate weddings, begin new business ventures, and even plan long journeys on akshaya tritiya.

This golden day falls on the third day of the bright half of the Hindu month of *baishakha* (April–May) when astrologically, the sun and the moon happen to be in exaltation and are simultaneously at the peak of their brightness, which occurs only once in a year. Nature's positive energies are hyperactive on this day, making each second of this day auspicious. It is hence a full mahurat day and if akshaya tritiya falls on *rohini nakshatra*, on a Monday, it becomes even more auspicious.

The myths around akshaya tritiya are that the day marked the beginning of the Treta Yuga (7000 BC), the second of the four yugas. According to the Puranas, sage Vedavyasa, along with Lord Ganesha, started writing the great epic Mahabharata on akshaya tritiya. According to another legend, when the Pandavas were in exile, Lord Krishna presented them on this day with an akshaya *patra*, a bowl which would never go empty, and would produce an unlimited supply of food on demand.

Perhaps the most famous of the akshaya tritiya stories is the legendary friendship between Lord Krishna and his poor Brahmin friend Sudama. On this day, as the tale goes, Sudama came over to Krishna's palace in Dwarka to request him to redeem his poverty. However, Sudama could not bring himself to make this particular request to Krishna. After spending the day together and reliving happy moments of their childhood days, Sudama returned home the next day to find that in place of his humble hut stood a magnificent palace, his wife looking resplendent in fine clothes and jewellery, and his children dressed likewise. Fine artifacts, furniture, gemstones and servants too added glamour to his new and beautiful house. Sudama realized that although he hadn't been able to voice his innermost desire, the gracious Krishna had understood his predicament and blessed him thus.

Balarama Jayanti is also observed on this day. Lord Balarama is also referred to as one of the *dashavatara*s or ten incarnations of Lord Vishnu. Lord Parashurama is also said to have been born on akshaya tritiya.

The festival of akshaya tritiya is dedicated to Lord Vishnu. Worshipping Lord Vishnu on this day eradicates and removes sins, and makes one free from all sorrows. Tulsi water is sprinkled in the area immediate to the idol of Lord Vishnu while performing his *arati*. The Puranas state that devotees who perform the Sri Maha Vishnu puja on akshaya tritiya may attain salvation. In some regions, devotees fast on this day. As per the Puranas, giving away of hand fans or *pankhas*, rice, salt, ghee, sugar, vegetables, tamarind, fruits and clothes on akshaya tritiya is a very important aspect of the festival. In some regions of India, devotees perform tulsi puja on akshaya tritiya.

In Orissa, akshaya tritiya marks the advent of the agricultural season when farmers start cultivating their land, while construction of chariots for the *rath yatra* begins at Puri. In Bengal, *hal-khata*, a ceremony involving the use of new audit books, is performed with the worship of Ganesha and Goddess Lakshmi. Bengalis perform many rites and rituals on this day.

Akshaya tritiya is generally observed by fasting and worshipping Lord Vasudeva, another form of Lord Vishnu, with rice grains. A dip in the river Ganges on this day is considered to be favourable.

The trend nowadays, however, is to spend this propitious day in purchasing gold and diamonds rather than observing fast or doing charity or pujas. Gold and diamond dealers do brisk business by offering alluring rebates on purchases on this day.

Shivaratri: The Night to Receive Shiva's Blessings

In ancient Indian tradition, the night is considered more conducive than the day for spiritual sadhana. The *navaratri*s for Shakti puja, Diwali for Lakshmi puja, and Holi for mantra siddhis are such special and well-known nights of the Hindu calendar. These nights are auspicious because a certain astronomical configuration occurs annually at this time of the year.

Scientifically too the nights are regarded better than days because during the day, the sun's rays cause resistance to earthly vibrations to rise higher into the outer space. This is the reason why yogis prefer to do their sadhana during the night hours so that the vibrations emanating from their sadhana mantras can drift upward to the desired higher planes of the astral world. It is commonly experienced that radio signals are received and heard better during nights because of the absence of sun's rays.

On account of the distinct astronomical occurrence, certain favourable divine vibes, obviously invisible but in abundance, descend on earth from Shivalok, one of the spheres of the outer space, on the night of Shivaratri, to bless devotees who remain awake and pray to Shiva during that night with a focused mind.

It may surprise many to know that there are in all twelve Shivaratris, one in each month of the Hindu calendar. The Shivaratri falling on the 13th/14th night during the *krishna paksha*, in the Hindu month of *phalguna*, is, in fact, the Maha Shivaratri, which normally falls in February or early March, as per the Gregorian calendar. On this day, the planetary position in the northern hemisphere acts as a potent catalyst to help a person raise his spiritual level. It is also believed that the gains or benefits that one receives from the recitation of Lord Shiva's death-averting mahamantra, the *maha mrityunjaya*, are received manifold by devotees on this night.

Traditionally, the ideal time for performing Shiva puja on Shivaratri is the *nishith* kaal. It is during this time that Lord Shiva appeared on earth in the form of a lingam. In south India, on this day, the most auspicious *lingabhava* puja is performed in all Shiva temples.

The important components of Shivaratri are rigid fasting for twenty-four hours and sleepless vigil during the night, singing songs in Shiva's praise, doing kirtan or collective singing, chanting aloud '*Om namah Shivaya*' and '*Har har Mahadev*'. A true devotee of the Lord spends the night in deep meditation while observing a fast and keeping a vigil. Because of the distinctive planetary position in the sky during the night of Shivaratri, there is a natural upsurge of divine

energy in the human system of those who are awake
and focused on Shiva, which is beneficial for one's
physical and spiritual well-being.

There are certain rituals, according to the *Shiva
Purana*, associated with Shivaratri:

- *Abhisheka* or bathing of the Shiva lingam with
  holy water, milk, curd and honey. This act of the
  devotee ensures purification of his own soul.
- Application of *vibhuti* and vermillion on the
  lingam and placing of wood apple and *belpatra*.
  This act is aimed at receiving virtue.
- Lighting a lamp with ghee made from cow milk
  in front of the lingam for attaining knowledge.
- Burning of incense in front of the lingam for
  attaining wealth.
- Offering betel leaves on the lingam to gain
  satisfaction from worldly pleasures.
- Offering seasonal fruits on the lingam for
  contributing to longevity and gratification of the
  devotees' desires.

It is believed that Lord Shiva is constantly burning with
the fire of austerity. Therefore, of all the above rituals,
the abhisheka pleases Shiva the most. Hence, only such
items are offered to him that have a cooling effect such
as coconut water, Gangajal, ghee, honey, milk, curd and
water from the seven seas or seven rivers.

As on Shivaratri, the Shiva tatwa or the vibrations
from Shivalok descend on earth to bless his devotees.
Similarly, on Guru Purnima day, which falls on the

day of purnima or full moon in the month of *ashadha* (June–July), the guru tatwa or radiations from the planet Jupiter descend on earth. The guru tatwa is said to be a thousand times more active on this day than on any other. People go to their true spiritual guru and perform guru puja to receive his blessings.

In both cases, Shivaratri and Guru Purnima, faith in the tradition and sincerity in performing the rituals with a focused mind are of paramount importance.

15

The Divine Alchemy of Kumbh

The tradition of kumbh mela is most ancient in India. It is older than Lord Rama and Krishna. The roots of this ritual are deeply connected to man's inborn craving for happiness, prosperity, fame, good health, well-being, enlightenment and immortality. The Vedas, Puranas, and other texts are full of references to it. Enlightened saints and sadhus tell us that most Puranic tales are written in a code language through which universal truths are revealed to laymen.

The kumbh too can be traced back to one such tale, which is associated with the *samudra manthan* or the churning of the ocean. This event is described as an alchemical process through which the first to emerge was poison, which was consumed by Lord Shiva, followed by mind-boggling divine attributes of health, wealth, beauty, power, auspiciousness and immortality in the form of nectar or *amrit* that surfaced from the sea. Samudra manthan is considered the source for the origin of kumbh.

When amrit rose from the ocean, Vishwakarma, the divine architect, created a magnificent kumbh or pot to contain it. This amrit kumbh attracted all who were present. A struggle of epic proportions ensued between the *sura*s or *deva*s or divine beings and *asura*s or demonic beings for the amrit kumbh as they all wanted to drink from it and become immortal. During the battle, a few drops of amrit spilled at four different places, at four different times. The kumbh mela is, therefore, celebrated at those four places when the same zodiacal position repeats itself.

The moon, the sun, Jupiter and Saturn — all teamed up to protect the amrit kumbh from the asuras. The moon helped in preventing the amrit from spilling out; the sun helped by protecting the kumbh from splitting or breaking; Jupiter prevented the asuras from snatching and fleeing with the amrit kumbh; while Saturn assisted the sun by instilling the fear of Indra — the king of the devas — in the minds of the asuras.

The sun, who is ruled by agni tatwa or fire element, and the moon, who is ruled by the *soma* tatwa or water element, together control the activities of the entire universe. Both the microcosm and macrocosm are sustained by agni tatwa and soma tatwa. Our entire metabolism, catabolism and anabolism are sustained by the sun and the moon, which are represented in the physical body as two very important *nadi*s or flows of energy — the *pingala* and the *ida*. These two nadis are essential not just for the physical and mental activities of man but for his spiritual enlightenment as well. This clearly explains why, in the story of samudra manthan, the sun and the moon are depicted as the foremost protectors of the kumbh.

As per the story, when the amrit kumbh was carried by the gods, some amrit fell off from the kumbh at Haridwar, Allahabad, Nashik and Ujjain. These planetary positions recur after a lapse of six years and twelve years and that is when the *ardha* or half kumbh and *purna* or full kumbh are held. These four places are: Prayag, where the Ganga, Yamuna and Saraswati confluence; Ujjain, where flows the river Shipra; Nashik, where originates the river Godavari; and Haridwar, where the Ganga touches the plains when coming down from the mountains.

The kumbh is held at Prayag, in Allahabad, when Jupiter enters Aries, and the sun and moon enter Capricorn. In Haridwar, at the foothills of the Himalayas, the festival is held when Jupiter is in Aquarius and the sun is in Aries. It is held at Ujjain, in Madhya Pradesh, when Jupiter is in Leo and the sun in Aries. In Nashik, in Maharashtra, the kumbh is held when both Jupiter and sun are in Leo.

The maha kumbh is held every twelve years as the struggle between the divine beings and the demons for the amrit kumbh lasted for twelve days, which equal twelve human years. The exact period of the kumbh is determined by nakshatra or constellation, tithi or day as per the lunar calendar, and the movement of planets to form special alliances. According to the calculations of astrologers and astronomers, the exact position that the planets had held during the samudra manthan, when the drops of amrit fell, occurs once in every twelve years. Lakhs of devotees take a dip in the waters of these rivers at the kumbh mela as during that period, a nexus of cosmic energies converges at that spot and charges the waters, bringing a dramatic change in the destiny of the devotees.

Kumbh: The Redeemer of Sins

Besides the spiritual, cultural, sociological, ecological and economic significance, the kumbh mela is also a very important event from the psychological point of view. Although every man is essentially pure and untainted, he knowingly or unknowingly sins and is often riddled with guilt during the course of his life. This causes severe aberration in his personality, relationships, lifestyle and mental outlook. The feeling of having sinned is very difficult to erase. No amount of counselling, reasoning, or medical treatment can reach those areas of the mind where sin and guilt lie hidden.

Sin is not an act: it is a deeply rooted notion or belief. Crime is an act and it is defined by law. But what about the thought of having sinned? How can that be handled? One is struck by the guilt of sin if the notion of past karma is attached to this idea. This is far more difficult to manage. It is in this area of psychological treatment that the kumbh works wonders. The same wonder works behind the

Christian practice of 'confession', which eradicates the feeling of guilt.

People also go to the Ganga to seek forgiveness for their sins, imaginary or real. Since time immemorial, the majestic and peaceful Ganga has held the power to absorb and wash away the sins of all who bathe in her waters. These include sins committed in past lives that we are not even aware of, but which are embedded in the deeper layers of our consciousness in seed form as *samskara*s. The purity of Ganga absorbs all these and it is for this reason that a dip at the kumbh enables man to churn his karmas or perform manthan karma, whereby the speed of his evolution is hastened.

Today, ecologists all over the world are trying to generate awareness about the need for conserving the environment. If we do not pay heed to their warnings, we stand to lose many things, including the chance to live. The tsunami of 2005 was one such act of nature that warned man of the consequences of taking nature for granted. The tradition of kumbh should impress ecologists as it achieves just what they are trying to do. Man does not learn through dictums and laws: he has a natural inclination to revolt against them. He follows them only out of fear. Fear does not transform an individual; it only keeps his baser instincts in abeyance till such time when he can do what he wants. Our rishis and munis understood the inherent nature of man. They were the original ecologists. They gave man a reason to worship nature by sanctifying it and revealing its role in the evolution of mankind. Handed down from generation to generation, this belief has become a part of India's psyche and inherent faith.

It is said that during the period of kumbh, apart from all the divine beings, all astral rishis and munis assemble to bless us. Their presence, together with the planetary conjunctions, surcharges the atmosphere, creating an energy field to redeem us from our sins.

The kumbh is the largest congregation of its kind known to man, for which it has found a place in the *Guinness Book of Records*. The mela is not for Hindus alone; it is for anyone and everyone who desires happiness, prosperity, good health and enlightenment. It is thus a secular event for all mankind.

In yoga too we find reference to the kumbh. In the practice of *pranayama*, there is a term called *kumbhakavastha*. This is that state when breath is neither drawn in nor expelled but is held suspended within. This is the main part of pranayama through which *prana shakti* or the life force is transformed as well as channelled, and the dissipating tendencies of the mind are destroyed — a sort of mental manthan or churning of the mind.

Ancient civilizations paid obeisance to all forms of nature, including ravens. Many cultures have now lost this awareness. Vedic literature is abundant with the most beautiful prayers to rivers, trees, the air and all other life-giving attributes of Mother Nature. This is because the Vedas believe that nature is not inert; it moves, it listens, it feels and it speaks — because it has many things to tell. But most importantly, it creates energy fields, which we can avail of through worship, love and care.

This acknowledgement of the sentience of nature is an essential part of all Vedic and tantric scriptures.

The Vedic lineage believed that man does not have proprietary rights to knowledge; rather, he is only its guardian. He is the preserver, not the owner. The knowledge that in the kumbh, certain planetary conjunctions charge a particular area and waterbody with divine energy was known to Vedic seers long ago.

Rishis of great spiritual power such as Yajnavalkya, Bharadwaja, Vashishtha and Vishwamitra bathed at Prayag. Even today, sadhus and householders observe *kalpa vaas* or a month-long vow at Prayag during kumbh. For this period, they have their abode on the banks of the Ganga and follow strict observances. One of the great emperors of India, Harshavardhana, who lived in the early seventh century (AD 606–38), patronized the kumbh mela and also performed kalpa vaas at Prayag. He gave away all his wealth and assets to the poor, slept like a beggar on the bare floor during his stay at Prayag, and returned to his kingdom empty-handed.

The Hindu genius had the firm belief that a bath at the kumbh is no ordinary event, as it removes obstacles in man's progress towards supreme achievements in his life. But to receive the intended result, a correct and untainted approach has to be taken. Sadly, such an approach is impractical in our present-day life where time flies faster than a jet.

16
Significance of Navratri

Navratri means 'nine auspicious nights'. During this period of nine nights, different forms of Goddess Durga, the cosmic female energy, is worshipped. Ma Durga, as she is popularly referred to, is the amalgam of the effulgence of all the major gods, including the Hindu trinity of Brahma, Vishnu and Maheshwar. The Devi is beautiful, bountiful, terrifying, compassionate and ruthlessly righteous. She is Durga and Kali in Bengal, Ambika and Bhadrakali in Gujarat, Vaishnodevi in Jammu and Kashmir, Chamunda in Karnataka, Santoshi Ma and Bhavani in Maharashtra, and Kamakhya in Assam. To most of us, she is just 'Ma', the Universal Mother.

The 700 verses of the *Devi Mahatmyam*, also called *Durga Saptashati* of *Markandeya Purana*, is recited daily during the navratris. The mantras invoking Ma Durga are repeated using a *haldi* mala or turmeric garland. She is hailed as the very origin of all the worlds. As per Hindu thought, there are three worlds and she is hailed as the originator of all the three as the female energy which gives birth to creations in the world. She is said to have all the three *gunas* of *satva, rajas* and *tamas* — purity, passion and inertia.

The ancient Indian social scientists — the rishis and munis — held certain nights of the year to be more conducive for practising spiritual sadhanas as compared to days. Some of these special nights are the nights of Dipawali, Shivratri and Holi. These nights and the nine nights of navratris are very special for spiritual growth and also for carrying out black magic practices.

Why are these nights so special, particularly, the navratris? The reason is that they fall during the time when the astrological and astronomical position of our country in the Milky Way is such that it allows our prayers and sadhanas to reach astral regions faster and without being distorted. Modern science also acknowledges that all human thoughts have electromagnetic energy. After sunset and during night, nature releases our thought energy into the astral region and it returns duly charged around dawn. During the day, due to the sun's rays, our thought energy cannot rise high enough into the atmosphere, hence nights are more suited. During the navratris, however, our thoughts rise higher into the astral world as compared to other nights.

The navratris occur twice in a year. The first is at the onset of the Vikrama era, the Hindu calendar followed in north India, in the month of chaitra from the first tithi or day of the shukla paksha of the month up to *navami*, the ninth day. The second occurrence comes exactly six months later, just before the winter. Thus, the two navratris fall at the time of the turning of seasons when the sun's rays are mild and soft, and they cannot much distort the thought energy. Spiritual practice during the navratris, when sincerely carried out, reach the desired destination faster.

Navratris have another aspect that makes them significant. It is a phenomenon of nature that when seasons change, the inner chemistry of human beings also changes. Observing fast during these periods keeps one healthy. The navratris provide people a religious reason to observe fast which helps one to gain at two levels: one at the physical level, and the other at the subtle spiritual level.

RITUALS: PUJAS AND YAGNAS

17

Why Are Yagnas Performed?

Yagna or *havan* is an integral part of Vedic culture. The worship of fire has a deep philosophy behind it. The Aryans wrote the Vedas and the first word in the Rig Veda is agni or fire.

Yagna is based on the science of agni. According to the science of fire, whatever substance we offer into it is reduced to ashes, and its subtle elements turn gaseous and expand to soar high into the atmosphere and beyond. Before offering any article or substance into the havan *kund*, the pit made into the ground or made of metal for the purpose of making offerings to the god of fire, it is charged with a mantra and thus guided towards a particular deity by naming it. Our oblations are consequently received by the forces of nature. Like the ancient rishis, NASA (National Aeronautics and Space Administration) scientists have also discovered that substances expand when heated. These scientists observed that when they fired rockets, the volume of the pre-recorded voices in the missiles automatically increased (Source: *Kundalni Aghora-II* by Robert E. Savoda, p. 33, 1993, Rupa & Co), which confirmed the truth in the ancient belief that things enlarge when they burn.

Mantras and the havan kund were two important constituents of fire worship in olden days, when havan kunds were prepared after due deliberations, and with great care. The size and shape of a havan kund differed from person to person. The shape and size of bricks to be used for preparing the havan kund were in accordance with the vital statistics of the person who would perform the yagna, after employing the principles of Vedic mathematics and geometry.

As per the maxims of ancient geometry, there were ten different shapes and sizes of havan bricks. The maxims of ancient geometry known as *Sublabha Sutra* are very old and date back to the eighth century BC. In 1975, a yagna based purely on ancient tradition was performed in Kerala for which one thousand bricks were used to construct the havan kund. It was reported that the yagna produced the desired result (*Week*, August 1975).

Pieces of wood, ghee, herbs, grains and other articles used for offering into the fire are chosen very carefully. All the selected items are not only eco-friendly, but also air purifiers. And once these substances are reduced to ashes, they turn into a potent medicine and are distributed to devotees as *bhasma prasadam* which is applied on the forehead, and a pinch of the holy ash is consumed. The wood of only such trees and plants is used which does not emit poisonous gases and the resultant ash is agreeable to human beings when consumed or applied on the person. Only ghee made from cow milk, specified herbs, dry fruits and some other articles are offered into the fire while conducting a yagna.

Besides these, certain favourite items of a particular deity are also offered to the fire, e.g., pieces of sugar cane are offered in Ganesha havan, while *kheer*—a milk and rice pudding—is offered in Vishnu havan. Linseeds are offered in the havan held for ancestors. These articles are consigned to the fire after reciting the name of a particular deity or ancestor. These substances are reduced to gases and ash by the fire. Since astral bodies have a very keen sense of smell, they accept our offerings in the form of fragrance and odour.

There are certain rules and restrictions for both the priest conducting the yagna and the person performing it. Both have to abide by the prescribed code of conduct: maintain celibacy, avoid getting angry, speak less, sleep on the floor, control intake of food, and so on. The science behind such a code is that it makes a man physically receptive and sensitive to divine blessings and to conserve energy.

In ancient days, the festival of Holi was a collective yagna performed by the entire community of a village on the full moon night of the Hindu month of phalguna. Holi marked the end of winter and the advent of summer. The Holi yagna was intended to purify the atmosphere. It is believed that the fumes of cow dung fire protect people against harmful radiations. According to certain scholars, it was a special day for fire worshippers. Only cow dung cakes were used to make a fire and dry fruits, tender grains of wheat and green grams were offered to it. The yagna fire, unlike today, was ignited not through any matchstick, but through mantras. The bonfire was lit exactly when the moon attained its full glory of purnima. The precise moment was calculated by astrologers using Vedic mathematics.

The present character of this festival has radically changed, and what we see today is only its corrupted and distorted form. In the olden days, curd, cow dung and colours extracted from vegetables and flowers were used to play Holi, unlike today, when chemical colours are used, with severe side effects.

18

Why Is a *Kalash* Installed Ceremoniously during a Puja?

The kalash or pot plays a significant role in most of our rituals and pujas. Also known as kumbh in certain parts of the country, it is a pot made of brass, copper, or clay that is filled with water from seven rivers, seven wells, or seven seas. The pot could even be filled with water from any single source or filled with unbroken grains of rice together with nine or eleven mango leaves surrounding a coconut placed on its top. Red or white cotton thread is tied around the pot in an intricate diamond-shaped pattern, and the pot may even be decorated with auspicious signs and designs.

A kalash is placed with due rituals before all important auspicious occasions like weddings, *grihapravesh* — the house-warming ceremony — and navratri puja. It is also ceremonially used while receiving holy personages. Sometimes, a kalash is placed near the entrance of the house to welcome honoured guests.

According to legend, before the world was created, Lord Vishnu lay reclining on his *sheshanaga shaiyya* or serpent bed in *Ksheersagar* or the milky ocean. A lotus emerged from his naval and from this lotus, Lord Brahma, the creator of this world, appeared. The water in the kalash symbolizes the primordial water from which Lord Brahma and the entire creation came into existence. The coconut fruit placed at its mouth represents the head of the devotee. The mango leaves arranged around the coconut are meant to attract divine vibrations from the astral world to bless the devotee and to divinize the water or the rice filled in the kalash. When rice is filled in it, it is called *purnakalash*. The rice that is filled in the pot is known as *akshat* or unbroken grains of rice, symbolizing eternal blessings on the devotee and his family. The akshat—that which will not exhaust—rice has the unique quality of being able to absorb the negativity that is in the environs. The kalash is, therefore, considered auspicious, and is worshipped. While worshipping the kalash, the blessings of all the seven rivers and deities, including those of Lord Vishnu, are invoked. After the puja, its water is used for all the rituals, including the abhisheka or divine bath.

The consecration of an idol or of a temple carried out using the kalash is called kumbh abhisheka, and is done in a grand manner with elaborate rituals, including the pouring of holy water from one or more kalash over the head of the idol or the *shikhar* or dome of the temple.

19

What Is the Significance of Lighting a Lamp while Performing Rituals?

In all religions of the world, 'light' universally symbolizes both the Almighty and knowledge. It is the very source of all life in the universe and, therefore, light is worshipped as the Supreme Lord himself, the enlivener and illuminator of all knowledge. Similarly, just as light removes darkness, knowledge dispels inner ignorance. True knowledge is an unending, ever-growing wealth by which all outer objects can be acquired. Hence, we light a lamp to bow down to and acknowledge light and knowledge as the greatest of all forms of being that exist on this planet.

In traditional Indian homes, a lamp filled with pure ghee is lit daily before the altar of the Lord. In some houses, it is lit at dawn; in some twice a day, at dawn and dusk. In certain homes, it is kept lit twenty-four hours of the day. Such a lamp is known as *akhanda* jyoti or *deepam*. All auspicious functions commence with the lighting of a lamp, which is considered as a propitious beginning for any ceremony.

When a lamp filled with pure ghee from cow milk is lit, it attracts divine or positive vibrations from the atmosphere and divinizes the place. This ghee, on evaporating, has the potency to attract positive vibrations which is its unique property. It is for this reason that only ghee lamps should be lit for gods and on auspicious occasions. But, nowadays, we are unmindful of this tradition and use oil instead. Oil lamps are used for the arati of a person and not of a deity as oil has the property to ward off negativity but does not attract divine vibrations. When a war hero returns, or when a bridegroom goes for marriage, the lady of the house performs his arati with an oil lamp to ward off the evil eye.

A lit lamp has a spiritual message. The ghee in it denotes human *vasana*s or desires and negative tendencies whereas the wick in it symbolizes man's ego. When it is outwardly lit—when a man mentally concentrates on the Supreme Lord—it is an inward action, but when he lights a lamp outside, it becomes an outward action; it removes negativity and attracts divinity. When it is lit within, through knowledge, it destroys the vasanas from their very root and gradually, the ego is decimated. The flame of a lamp always burns upwards and that inspires us to acquire such knowledge that will take us towards higher goals, ideals and noble deeds.

In traditional homes, a candle or bulb is not lit before the altar as it does not have the potency to create the desired effect. It is, however, an unpleasant truth of the modern age that we resort to short cuts as it is convenient but, in reality, these short cuts will not yield any tangible results except the psychological satisfaction of being religious.

According to a recent research (Source: 238th National Meeting of the American Chemical Society held in September 2007) carried out in the US, candles made from paraffin wax are harmful for humans. This is because the chemicals released by these candles discharge substances such as toluene and benzene, which cause cancer and can affect the nervous system.

However, beeswax candles, apparently, do not release harmful air pollutants and are comparatively safer.

Interestingly, thousands of years ago, Indian seers and saints studied in depth the effects of air pollutants released by lamps filled with different types of oils and ghee. They found that ghee from cow milk, mustard oil and coconut oil were agreeable to humans, in that order. Other oils were found to be unsuitable.

20
Why Do Hindus Perform the Arati?

There are sixteen items—*shodasha upachara*—in a puja and arati is one of these. Normally, arati is performed towards the end of ritualistic worship and also to welcome a holy person or an honoured guest. During a puja, the arati is always accompanied by the ringing the *ghanti* or bell, musical instruments, singing and clapping.

Arati for a deity is observed with a ghee lamp and camphor. This holds spiritual significance: when lit, camphor completely burns itself without leaving any trace of its existence, and this symbolizes complete decimation of one's ego or self. While the camphor burns, it emits a pleasant perfume. In our spiritual progress, as we serve the guru, parents, elders and society we too should willingly surrender ourselves so as to spread the perfume of love to all. This is the philosophical explanation of the ritual.

However, scientifically, there is a different explanation to it. The images in traditionally enshrined and celebrated temples where regular pujas are diligently performed according to scriptures have a definite divine aura around them. When the arati of such enshrined images is done, their aura expands due to heat and all those who are present receive divine vibrations and gain spiritual strength. For this reason, it is always advocated that one must attend the arati because the atmosphere in the temple is especially charged with enhanced positivity and one receives divine vibrations or blessings even without asking.

At the end of the arati, we place our palms over the arati flame, then gently touch our eyes and the top of our head. While doing so, we mentally pray: 'May the light that illuminated the Lord light up our intellect; may our vision be divine and our thoughts noble and well meaning.'

On the other hand, the arati of an individual is carried out for a different reason, with a different medium—oil—and on different occasions such as for a newly wed couple or a newly born child on his *namakaran* or naming ceremony, or a brother on the occasion of Bhai Dooj, a day when a sister goes to her brother's house to wish him well, or the husband on Karva Chauth, a day when a wife fasts for the long life of her husband, or hero when he returns from war. It is an established fact that all humans have an aura which may be affected by the evil eyes of jealousy, or by the negative thoughts of another person. Performing the arati of individuals wards off such ill effects. However, oil lamp is used for an individual's arati and not a ghee lamp. This is because oil, particularly of mustard and linseed, has the power to ward off negativity cast by the evil eye of another person. Ghee from cow milk, on the other hand, has the potency to enliven a god's image or idol.

21

Why Is *Paan–Supari* Used in Rituals?

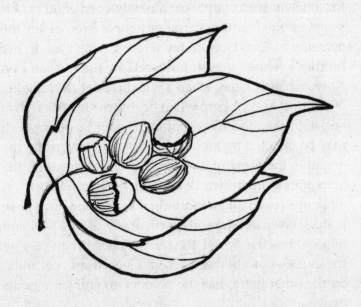

All Hindu rituals are carried out in serene surroundings, at a sanctified place, and conducted with pure objects. Most of the commodities used for the rituals are unique and with divine characteristics. Amongst several important objects, betel leaves or paan, together with areca nuts or supari are indispensable. Both are sacred and sanctified by nature. That is why they form an integral part of any ritual.

In Sanskrit literature, paan is referred to as *tambulam*. It is also called *nagavalli* in Sanskrit, which brings to mind the image of a creeper with the hood of a cobra. *Naga* means serpent in Sanskrit, and *valli* is a 'creeper'; hence, the name nagavalli. The sweet smelling leafy creeper, it is said, emerged from a sacred purna *ghata* or clay pot, which contained amrit or nectar when the sea was being churned by the gods and the demons. The gods outwitted the demons, obtained the pot, and consumed the nectar, but sent the pot down to earth. The tender and sacred nagavalli took root and flourished for human beings.

The paan creeper is very sensitive, tender and sacred. It is believed that if a lady goes near the betel crop during her menstrual cycle, it will soon rot and decay as it cannot withstand the odour. Nature has made the paan so very susceptible to strong smells.

Since the paan is sensitive, it draws both celestial and earthly vibrations. The stem of the leaves plays an important role in this function. A leaf without the stem at its end cannot attract any vibrations; the stem serves as the antenna of the leaf through which it receives outer vibrations. That is why a paan is offered to a deity keeping the stem towards the image of the Divine.

Ayurveda highlights many uses of the paan. It is used as a carminative, a digestive, and at the same time it is invigorating. The bride and bridegroom exchange the paan during their marriage for stimulation.

The areca nut or supari symbolizes the ego and the hard, coarse quality of man, which must be surrendered to the deity. There are two types of supari — one which is reddish and round, and the other which is oval and whitish. For rituals, the oval type is ideally suited because this is able to attract greater divine vibrations from the atmosphere. Both water and earth elements are divinely blended in the supari and this makes it effective for activating celestial vibrations. Rishis and munis listed only such objects of nature for puja that are commensurate with the Divine and have positive energy. The betel leaf and areca nut are two such extraordinary objects.

22

What Is the Significance of *Chandan* in Rituals?

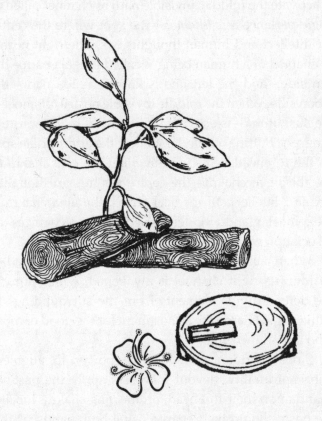

During different pujas and rituals, a paste made of chandan or sandalwood is invariably used to put a *tilak*, vermillion mark, on the forehead of the deity and devotees. Amongst the many substances used for tilak, chandan and *ashtagandha*, a powder of eight aromatic herbs, are the most satvik—pure and pious.

A chandan tilak is applied between the two eyebrows to activate the middle, invisible nadi or channel called in yogic parlance as *sushumna*—the spot where the centre for intellect and human thoughts lies. The right nostril or channel of a human being is called pingala nadi—the sun side—and the left one is known as ida nadi—the moon side. When the middle invisible nostril/channel—the sushumna—is activated, a man can make spiritual progress. Putting a chandan tilak at the appropriate spot on the forehead helps in enlivening the *ajna* chakra or the third-eye chakra—the centre for human thoughts, sex and intellect. In medical terms, the ajna chakra is the pineal gland. Modern science too recognizes its association with human thoughts and sexual urges.

When a chandan tilak is applied on the forehead of an idol, its right channel is awakened, which attracts the deity's divine elements from the surroundings to enliven and charge the atmosphere for the good of those who attend the ritual.

Since chandan tilak has the power to augment one's spirituality, devout followers apply the paste of chandan on their forehead, on the ajna chakra. Ideally, the paste should be prepared using both hands, as this activates one's Shiva–Shakti elements present in the right and left sides of the nostrils. The union of the two divine elements is conducive for the success of man.

As per ancient wisdom, after death, the human mind remains alive for a few hours. Modern science too endorses this view. According to the prescribed rituals for last rites, before the body is carried to the cremation ground, a chandan tilak is applied on the forehead of the deceased. But this paste is prepared using only the right hand. It is believed that such a paste charges the sun element of the pingala nadi that helps in activating the life force still left in the dead body.

When human body is cremated, it disintegrates into the five basic elements—panchabhootas—of nature. To hasten the process of disintegration, *kapala kriya* or the splitting of the skull is carried out by the person performing the last rites. This is a unique and scientific ritual carried out by the Hindus.

In olden days, the dead bodies of kings, celebrated seers, saints and people like the Buddha and the poet Kalidasa were cremated only on pyres of sandalwood. In recent history, Mahatma Gandhi, Pandit Jawaharlal Nehru and Indira Gandhi were cremated with chandan wood as it is pure and powerful, which helps in faster disintegration of a body. Those who cannot afford sandalwood place at least a few pieces of it on the pyre of the deceased for the same reason. After the death of a person, people garland his picture with a chandan mala to receive his spiritual blessings.

Unadulterated chandan paste has satvik elements that help to augment one's spirituality. However, when *kumkum*, turmeric powder, or saffron are mixed with chandan paste, its satvik potency is diluted because these three products are rajasik or passionate in their effects. That is why saints and those who pursue a spiritual life apply only pure white chandan paste on their forehead. However, those who lead a worldly life may apply chandan paste mixed with kumkum, turmeric, and/or saffron that gives them a twofold benefit.

Interestingly, the Parsis, in their Agyaris or fire temples burn pieces of chandan wood only. In their faith too chandan is considered pious and sacred, which creates divine vibrations in the surroundings.

23

Why Do Hindus Chant *Shanti* Three Times?

Peace and harmony are natural to nature and man. Where there is peace, there is happiness. However, we do come across people who seem to have everything—name, fame, financial stability, social stature, and good health—but are still not happy, content and at peace. This is because peace is of two types—internal and external. In spite of his apparent prosperity and success, a person may not be at peace with himself. This means that success in the material and physical world does not come with an assurance of peace. Hence, he yearns for it.

Man's peace is disturbed by his own fears and worries that arise within or because of his circumstances. The seers and sages of ancient India analysed the sources that disturbed man's mental equilibrium and found that all agitations, problems and sorrows originated from three sources. One, the unseen divine forces of nature over which man has little or no control, such as earthquakes, floods, hurricanes, storms, volcanic eruptions and so on. The second source comprises known factors like accidents, crimes, unhealthy human relations, lust, passion and jealousy. Man's past actions that have not been repaid by him in his previous births constitute the third source. This last disturbance to man's peace is due to *adhyatmik* or supernatural reasons.

In their search for peace, rishis of yore discovered the principle of *trivaram* satyam or 'that which is sincerely said thrice comes true'. Even in modern times, it is commonly seen that when we repeat something three times, it is to emphasize a point. For instance, in the court of law, a witness takes the oath saying: 'I shall speak the truth, the whole truth, and nothing but the truth.' In Islam, the word talaq is repeated thrice for divorce to be effective.

Having realized the truth in the principle of trivaram satyam, our great masters asserted that when we chant 'shanti' thrice, peace will prevail over the three sources that upset the balance in our life and affect our innate peace. Therefore, to restore peace, we chant '*Om shanti, shanti, shanti . . . hi*' while concluding a puja, an arati, or some other ritual.

The first utterance of the word is chanted aloud, addressing the unseen forces of nature. The second chant is softer, directed to our immediate surroundings and all those around us. The third chant is the softest, because it is meant for oneself: to re-address our past life's karmic debts. It is by chanting thus that we strive to regain out lost tranquillity.

24

Why Do Hindus Observe *Shradh* for Their Ancestors?

Respect and reverence for parents, teachers and elders are an integral part of Indian culture. Our veneration towards them is not limited to only the living but also includes the departed. According to Hindu scriptures, while several factors shape our overall worldly growth and well-being, three play a more significant role. In spiritual parlance, the endowments by the three are known as *rin*s or debts: one, the favours of gods and benedictions of nature is known as *deva-rin*; two, the contribution and blessings of one's teachers, gurus and ancient rishis is called *rishi-rin*; and three, the *pitri-rin*, the debt one owes to one's ancestors.

Being grateful to those who favour us is another characteristic of Indian culture. Everything that helps mankind should be revered and preserved. Nature gives light, air, water, food and habitat without our asking and that too free. Such grace and blessing of nature are a debt for mankind. We pay back this debt by holding regular havans to detoxify and keep the air pollution-free, and also by watering, planting, and protecting plants and trees. Similarly, we repay the rishi-rin by observing the social customs and traditions established by ancient rishis, the great social thinkers of the past, who laid the foundations of a stable and organized society.

We also owe a debt to our parents, grandparents and great-grandparents. After all, they brought us to this world to continue the lineage; their genes are part of our body system and their mental traits unknowingly influence our thinking. Moreover, the food and care they gave us while we were children helped us to stand on our own. Their contribution in our life is indeed a debt which we must pay back.

Ancient books assert that when any of our ancestors depart from this world unwedded or childless, or meet an untimely tragic death, their inwardly unfulfilled desires or longings do not allow them to detach from this world. Such a person is not totally liberated from this planet even after death and remains earth-bound. His departed soul fails to reach heaven and continues at a lower astral region called the Pitriloka, which is located below the Chandraloka, a region below heaven, in the form of a *pinda* or ball-like form. The presiding deity of Pitriloka is Lord Dattatreya, a minor incarnation of Lord Vishnu.

In case the descendants of such an unliberated soul do not offer *tarpan* on the tithi or day and date of his death during shradh, the period between the full moon and new moon night of the month of *ashwina* (September–October) his soul may turn hostile towards the family. This may cause regular loss of wealth, frequent deaths in the family, or birth of only female children. This disorder in the family is called *pitridosha*. To protect oneself from such calamity, pitri-rin has to be dutifully discharged.

Our concern and respect for the departed is brought forth through regular tarpan-arpan. Tarpan means offering water to our ancestors while reciting their names and appropriate mantras. 'Arpan' means preparing dishes that the deceased person relished, and offering the same to a true Brahmin on the day of his shraadh. A ball of boiled rice mixed with jwar or millet, flour, black sesame and *kusha* grass is also offered to birds in the form of a pinda. The pinda ball represents the soul of the departed ancestor. Alternatively, the pinda can be immersed into some flowing holy water. This offering is known as pinda-dana, which propitiates the unliberated soul. The pinda souls that reside in Pitriloka are limbless and without any stomach. But, they have a very keen sense of smell. By way of tarpan-arpan, through the aroma of the offered food, these souls get satiated. Therefore, whatever we offer to them should be pure, aromatic, fresh and clean and should be offered with faith and regard; only then do they accept our offerings.

Lord Yama bestowed a boon on mankind that 'whoever offers tarpan-arpan to his ancestors will receive their blessings'.

As a thanksgiving gesture, Hindus propitiate their ancestors during the *mahalaya paksha* or *sharada paksha* between the full moon and moonless nights of the *ashwin maas* — September–October. The significance of propitiating one's ancestors by such rituals is detailed in quite a few Puranas — the *Vishnu, Varaha, Vayu* and *Matsya Purana*. Both *Manusmriti* and the Mahabharata also explain the importance of shradh. It is believed that during the fortnight of the waning moon of the ashwin maas, the astral bodies of ancestors leave their abode, the Pitriloka, to spend the fortnight in their descendants' homes in Prithviloka or earth, and expect them to offer tarpan. Since astrologically and astronomically, the earth is closest to the moon during these fifteen days, all offerings reach our ancestors quickly. Scientifically, the period between 14 July and 13 January is known as dakshinayan or lack of sun. During these months of the year, the sun is below the equator, towards the South Pole. From 13 January, e.g., the day of makar sankranti, the sun starts its northward journey. It is believed that the dakshinayan period refers to a negative state of mind. The *chaturmas*, the first four months of dakshinayan — *ashadh*/June-July; *sawan*/July-August; *bhado*/August-September; and ashwin/September-October — have maximum negativity. During this period, no auspicious event is held by the Hindus, including marriages.

The negative state of mind in ashadha is related to anger; in shravana, to disturbed mind; in bhadra, to non-fulfilment of one's desires and uncontrolled ego; and in ashwina, it relates to the discontent arising from non-fulfilment of desires of our ancestors, particularly during amavasya. For this reason, shradhs are performed during ashwin maas.

It is believed that once shradh or pinda dana is successfully performed at Gaya, in Bihar, there is no need to perform the ritual thereafter. The only ritual that has to be performed is 'remembrance' on the shradh day, by doing some charity in their name.

Astrologically, the importance of Gaya is due to its geo-location on this planet. A prayer or a ritual carried out here is quite effective as it reaches its desired destination, provided it has been sincerely said and precisely performed.

The Crown Mantra: Gayatri

The Gayatri Mantra is the most revered mantra in the Vedic tradition. It is an invocation as well as a prayer addressed to the Supreme Creator of this universe and of the three worlds: the terrestrial, the celestial, and the one connecting these two. The literal meaning of the mantra is:

We meditate on the glory of that Ishwara—the Supreme Lord of the universe—who has created this universe and the entire cosmos, who is accomplished to be revered, who is the embodiment of true knowledge and light, who is the dispeller of all sorts of sins, who can destroy and dissolve our ignorance. May he enlighten our intellect.

When this mantra is correctly recited, it produces a large number of *taranga*s or alpha waves −1,10,000 alfa sound waves per second−in our mind that resonate in the region of the topmost cosmic energy centre called the *sahasrara* chakra or the crown chakra, in yogic parlance. Moreover, when the mantra is mentally recited without uttering its words aloud, its frequency is enhanced manifold and its potency increases tremendously, which greatly affects its chanter. It is believed that a person who chants the Gayatri Mantra 3,000 times each day at a particular place, sitting on the same seat at the same time, with the same mala or rosary, with a focused mind, for a period of forty days, is freed from his sins, however many they may be. The greatness of the mantra can be further gauged by the fact that not only the chanter but also its listener is divinely blessed. A man can repeat or chant the Gayatri Mantra mentally in any or all states while sitting, walking or even lying down; there is no commission or omission of any sort in doing so. Traditionally, however, the mantra is to be recited thrice; at sunrise, at solar noon and at dusk.

The efficacy of this mantra has been scientifically proven and proclaimed by Dr Howard Steingeril, an American scientist, who collected mantras, hymns and invocations from all religions of the world, and tested their potency in his physiology laboratory. He concluded that the Gayatri Mantra is the most rewarding, and is scientifically efficacious. This is the most powerful prayer hymn in the world. The combination of sound and the variation in the sound waves in their particular frequency is capable of developing specific spiritual potentialities. The Hamburg University also initiated the research into the efficacy of the Gayatri Mantra, both on the mental and physical planes. The Gayatri Mantra is now broadcast daily for fifteen minutes from 7 p.m. onwards, over Radio Paramaribo, Surinam, South America, for the past several years. In Amsterdam too the Gayatri Mantra is acknowledged as the most potent divine prayer hymn in the world.

The Gayatri Mantra has no author in the conventional sense. However, since it was revealed to brahmarshi Vishwamitra, he is the mantra *drashtar* or the one who first conceives or divinely receives a mantra. Gayatri, in fact, is the name of the meter in which the mantra is composed. It has three *pada*s or lines of eight syllables each, totalling to twenty-four syllables. However, according to the text as prescribed in the *Rig Veda Samhita* (3:62:10), the Gayatri Mantra has one syllable short; the first pada has seven syllables instead of eight. This shortage is compensated through an amended pronunciation of the word *varenyam* as *vareniyam*. There is yet another distinctive tenet about the Gayatri Mantra, that there are five pauses that one has to strictly observe while reciting it to receive the best from the mantra.

Every mantra has a presiding deity. In the case of the Gayatri Mantra, it is the sun god, Surya, also known as Savita. Surya is associated with Lord Vishnu, therefore, he who meditates on the Gayatri Mantra meditates on Lord Vishnu. Among the trinity, Vishnu is considered the most intelligent. Whenever the gods happen to be in trouble, they always run to Lord Vishnu to seek his advice. The Gayatri Mantra does the same to a man; it bestows the right wisdom for the seeker to sail through troubled waters.

During the Puranic age, the Gayatri Mantra was typically portrayed as a goddess seated on a red lotus flower, having a thousand petals on her five heads of

Mukta, Vidruma, Hema, Neda and Dhevala goddesses with their ten eyes looking into the eight directions, as also the earth and the sky. She holds in her ten arms all the weapons of Shiva, Vishnu and Brahma. Goddess Gayatri is also considered as an embodiment of goddesses Saraswati, Lakshmi and Parvati.

The benefits of regularly repeating the Gayatri Mantra are manifold. There is nothing more purifying for one's soul, either on this earth or in the heavens, than the Gayatri Mantra *japa* or repetition. It brings to one the same benefits as the recitation of all the Vedas put together, with their *anga*s — the limbs of the Vedas as auxiliary disciples associated with the study and understanding the Vedas; they are six in number: *shiksha*, *vyakarana*, *nirukta*, *chhanda*, *kalpa* and *jyoti*. A regular recitation of the mantra destroys all sins, bestows splendid health, wealth, beauty, vigour, physical strength, vitality and a divine aura on and around the face of its chanter. It also liberates one from the cycle of birth and death, and grants salvation.

The Gayatri Mantra is the mother of all the Vedas. Lord Krishna in the Gita asserts: 'Amongst the mantras, I am Gayatri.' The Gayatri is Brahma, the Gayatri is Vishnu, the Gayatri is Shiva, the Gayatri is all the Vedas; the Gayatri is thus the crown hymn of the Vedic tradition. Gayatri is not a mere cluster of words and letters but a letter capsule compacted with sound waves that created this universe. It is not a string of metered words alone; it, in fact, belongs to the science of acoustics that has far-reaching results.

TEMPLE RITUALS

25

Why Is a Coconut Offered in a Temple?

Our rishis and munis studied different plants and trees, and various other aspects of nature in depth. They found that the coconut was the most auspicious fruit, as it has the potency to draw divine vibrations from the outer world (Source: *Creation and Composition of the Universe*, Vol. 12, by Dr Jayant Balaji). For this reason, it is also known as *shriphal* or 'divine fruit'. When the coconut is broken by smashing it on the ground, one can hear a sound similar to that of the monosyllabic mantra, 'phut', which can ward off the ill effects of an evil eye.

The coconut is one of the most common offerings in a temple. The shape of this fruit is akin to a human head with three eyes. When it is to be offered to a deity, it should be offered with the eye side facing the deity as this is the sensitive side of the fruit that can receive divine vibes from the idol. According to legend, the coconut was created by the rishi Vishwamitra (Source: *Dharmick Va Samajik Krityon ka Adharbhoot Shastra*, Vol. 1, Dr Jayant Balaji Athavale, November 2005, Sanatana Santha ,Varanasi) for the well-being of humanity. When we offer a coconut at the feet of a deity, we symbolically offer our own head, implying total surrender to the Divine by detaching our ego from the self.

Coconut water, like Gangajal, is deemed sacred. It is sprinkled to remove the negativity of an affected area and also to purify a place. The white kernel of a broken coconut is later distributed to devotees as prasad. Coconut is also offered while undertaking a new venture, inaugurating a new bridge, building or dam, on buying a new vehicle, on entering a new house, during weddings, celebrating festivals, and so on. On concluding a havan, the purna *ahuti* or final offering is made by offering a ripe coconut into the sacrificial fire.

In Hindu society, the coconut enjoys immense economic importance also. Every part of this tree — the trunk, leaves, fruit and coir — is used in innumerable ways, either for making thatches, mats, tasty dishes, oil, soap or firewood. Its tree takes salty water from the earth and converts it into a sweet, nutritive drink that is especially beneficial for sick people. Its water is used in the preparation of many Ayurvedic medicines as also in other alternative medicinal systems.

During the traditional ritual of abhisheka carried out in temples, several items such as milk, curd, honey, sandalwood paste and holy ash are poured over the deity along with the water of a tender coconut. Each item used in the ritual bestows certain specific benefits on the devotees and coconut water is believed to bestow spiritual strength on the faithful.

26

Why Do Hindus Circumambulate a Deity in a Temple?

The Supreme Lord is the source centre and the essence of our lives. Recognizing him as the focal point of our lives, we go about doing our daily chores. This is the philosophical explanation of circumambulating—performig pradakshina or parikrama around—a deity. The true reason is that when we circumambulate a deity, we receive divine force because the idol constantly emanates energy in all directions. When we go around the image, we receive that exalted power from all directions and thus rejuvenate ourselves to face the challenges of life. It is, however, true of only such images that are properly, regularly, and sincerely worshipped by noble priests with pure minds and thoughts.

There is a correct and established way to do the pradakshina: it has to be done clockwise, always keeping the deity on our right side. In Indian philosophy, the right side symbolizes auspiciousness and, therefore, as we circumambulate, we keep the sanctum sanctorum on our right side and receive energy. There is another reason for going clockwise: as per the law of nature, the present moves to the future from left to right—the movement of time in a clock is from left to right; even the earth moves from left to right. Thus, devotees circumambulate from left to right of the main idol to receive divine blessings and strengthen themselves spiritually.

Besides deities, Indian scriptures advise that we must consider our parents and teachers also as the Lord. With this in mind, we should also do pradakshina around our parents, teachers and extraordinary personages to receive their blessings.

Another traditional practice is that after completion of special pujas, we customarily do pradakshina around ourselves too by rotating on the spot. In this way, we recognize and remember the Divine within us—*aham brahmasmi*—I am the Supreme Being.

27

Why Do Hindus Bathe before *Darshan* of a Deity in a Celebrated Temple?

When we reach a *dham* or celebrated shrine after travelling a long distance, we inadvertently gather negative energy en route. This inevitable situation disturbs our aura. If we go straightaway to the temple in that unclean state, we may not receive full blessings of the deity due to our disturbed aura. This is the reason why we are advised to bathe before taking a glimpse or darshan of the deity. In south India, most temples have ponds outside the shrine where devotees can bathe before offering their respects to the deity. Some devotees visit the temple with their wet clothes because wet clothes attract energy instantly. Some devotees don silk dhotis or saris as silk helps in generating positive energy.

In Islam, similar religious beliefs are prevalent, such as the practice of *wazoo* or washing one's hands and feet before entering the mosque's main area. For this purpose, a tank or taps are provided for the devotees to clean themselves. Even in Zoroastrianism, a similar practice is observed.

In the olden days, people were not allowed to enter Hindu kitchens with footwear, as these are carriers of negativity. Likewise, people were advised to wash their feet every time they returned home from outside. In those days, people mostly walked barefoot.

The same principle of negativity is behind the practice of taking a bath after returning home from the cremation ground, on attending someone's last rites.

28

Why Are Temple Doors Closed during an Eclipse?

It has been found that during an eclipse, heavenly bodies, particularly the sun and the moon, emit abnormal negative radiations. An idol, which has been ceremoniously and ritually installed, constantly emanates positive energy in clockwise direction from its being. During an eclipse, the clockwise cycle of the aura around the idol is somewhat disturbed. Therefore, the doors of the temple housing the main deity are closed to prevent and minimize these negative radiations that disturb divine energy.

In addition to closing temple doors, tulsi leaves are placed on the idols to safeguard them against radiation and negativity. Tulsi leaves are specifically chosen for this purpose as they have the capacity to absorb harmful radiations.

29

Why Is the Cooking of Food and Eating Prohibited during an Eclipse?

Science has proved that during an eclipse, there is enhanced radiation of ultraviolet and other rays that contaminate food. Obviously, the consumption of such food will be harmful for us. Although there may not be any immediate and apparent reaction, in due course of time, our teeth or digestive system are affected. Cooked food is affected as it contains water, and during an eclipse, water attracts more radiations, which in turn contaminate the food. To prevent this, tulsi leaves are placed on cooked food to repel radiations.

Pregnant women are advised not to cut vegetables or fruits, or use a metal implement such as a knife or a pair of scissors, during an eclipse. This is because the expectant woman attracts more radiations as the metallic object serves as a good conductor, thereby enhancing the possibility of some adverse impact on the fetus.

Since ancient times, people have been advised not to look at the sun with naked eyes during an eclipse because it may damage the retina of the eyes and lead to blindness. This age-old taboo is now supported by doctors and scientists. Special glasses are now used to view the sun when an eclipse is in progress.

TRADITIONS

30

Why Do Hindus Put a Tilak on Their Forehead?

Tilak is applied on the spot that lies between our eyebrows—the ajna chakra—which is the seat of all human thoughts and past memories. While applying the tilak, one prays, 'I remember the Almighty; may pious feelings pervade in all my activities; may I be righteous in my deeds.' The tilak thus seeks the Almighty's blessings, and serves as a guard against negative forces.

It is an established scientific fact that the entire human body emanates energy in the form of electromagnetic waves. Ajna chakra does so all the more vigorously. That is why when one is tense or anxious, a great deal of body heat is generated that gives one a headache. This biological fact was realized by our great seers and saints thousands of years ago. They, therefore, devised a method to safeguard this spot on the forehead as also to prevent loss of energy. After intense study and research, they found that sandalwood or chandan paste, turmeric and *kesar* or saffron are quite effective if applied on the ajna chakra. The individual will remain calm and controlled, with no undue energy loss.

However, there is a spiritual explanation too. The tilak invokes a feeling of sanctity in the wearer and also in the onlooker. It is considered a religious mark, and its shape and colour varies according to one's caste, religious sect and the deity one worships.

In ancient times, the four castes or varnas—Brahmin, Kshatriya, Vaishya and Sudra—applied the tilak differently. Brahmins applied the white sandalwood tilak, symbolizing purity, as their vocation was priestly and academic in nature. Kshatriyas applied red kumkum—a mixture of turmeric and lemon juice or lime signifying valour since they belonged to the warrior class. The colour red denotes valour and hyperactivity. Vaishyas wore a yellow tilak of sandalwood paste mixed with kesar or turmeric; the colour yellow signifies wisdom and foresight, which are essential for business acumen. Sudras wore a tilak of black bhasma or ash or charcoal, indicating service as they supported the work of the other three classes.

Further, Vaishnavites wear a chandan tilak in 'U' shape, whereas Shaivities have a *tripundra* or three horizontal lines across the forehead drawn with bhashma. Devi worshippers (or Shakthas) apply a red dot of kumkum.

31

What Is the Significance of Bhasma—Holy Ash?

Bhasma or vibhuti is the holy ash retrieved from the havan kund or sacrificial fire into which special logs of wood obtained from certain sacred trees, pure ghee, herbs and grains are offered, duly charged with mantras, to a deity. Ash obtained from this sacred fire is unique: it has immense potency, both spiritual as well as material.

Unlike other gods, Lord Shiva is additionally worshipped by pouring ash as abhisheka, and later, it is distributed to devotees as vibhuti. This bestows blessings to one who applies it on his forehead and other body parts. It also protects the wearer from ill health and the evil eye.

Vibhuti obtained from a sacred havan kund serves as divine herbal medicine. Applying vibhuti on different parts of the body can bring transcendental positive energy from the astral world. It is also a tool to enhance our body's receptivity. When applied at different body points, especially points of greater receptivity such as the ajna chakra, we receive greater divine energy.

Vibhuti is always taken with the ring finger because it is one of the most sensitive and sacred points of the body. To receive maximum benefit, apply vibhuti on the ajna chakra, the spot between the eyebrows; on the *vishuddha* chakra or throat chakra, the pit of the throat, to enhance speech power; on the *anahata* chakra or heart chakra, the centre of the chest; and just behind the earlobes. Men can apply a little vibhuti on their right big toe where the body's longest nerve ends while women should apply it on their left big toe.

The word 'bhasma' means 'that by which our sins are destroyed'. Bhasma is especially associated with Lord Shiva who is believed to apply it all over his body. Shaivites apply it on their forehead as tripundra or three parallel horizontal lines. When a kumkum dot is applied at the centre of the tripundra, the mark symbolizes Shiva—Shakti—the unity of energy and matter that creates the entire seen and unseen universe. Some devotees apply it on different parts of their body such as upper arms, chest and throat. Ascetics rub it all over their body, especially those who maintain a *dhuni* or eternal fire. Many devotees also consume a pinch of it each time they receive it to redeem their sins and mitigate their physical sufferings.

32

Why Do Hindus Wear a *Janeyu*?

A janeyu is a string made up of a number of consecrated threads to be worn by orthodox male Hindu Brahmins, Kashtriyas and Vaishyas. However, the type of janeyu differs from caste to caste and community to community. Brahmins, Kashtriyas and Vaishyas wear threads made out of cotton, hemp and wool, respectively.

The *upanayana* samskara or sacred thread ceremony is generally observed between the ages of seven and fourteen. In case the ceremony does not take place due to some reason during this age period, then it has to be performed before the marriage of the individual. The purpose of this ceremony is to prepare a young man to share the responsibilities of his elders. The thread is worn by the male in the company of a group of Brahmins chanting the Gayatri Mantra. The thread is twisted in an upward direction. The ceremony heralds that the wearer of the janeyu can hereafter actively participate in family rituals.

Brahmins use a janeyu with three strands, which stand for the Hindu trinity of Brahma, Vishnu and Mahesh. Others interpret it as the symbol of Mahasaraswati, Mahalakshmi and Mahakali. Many people believe it to be related with the past, present and future. Out of all such opinions, the most appropriate is that the three strands stand for ida, pingala and sushumna nadis, through which the *kundalini shakti* or hidden energy operates in a human body.

A janeyu is generally made of pure cotton strands. Cotton seeds have seven layers. In a human body too there are seven sheaths and also seven chakras. Therefore, pure cotton is spiritually compatible with the human body. This, however, is yet to be established by contemporary science. Before being worn, a janeyu is charged with appropriate mantras and is further sanctified by applying sandalwood paste and by soaking it in unboiled cow milk. Such a janeyu works on a person as an antenna to receive divine vibrations, particularly when it is maintained by following the prescribed instructions and code.

According to Ayurveda, a nerve called *lohitika* goes to the urinary track passing through the region of the right ear. When one slightly presses this nerve, the urinary track opens easily and the person is able to pass urine fully, thus throwing out toxins from his body. For this reason, Hindu males wind up the janeyu over their right ear to press this nerve while urinating. The lohitika nerve is also connected to the testicles and helps in checking hernia. Incidentally, modern doctors pierce the right ear lobe to check the growth of hernia in a man. Thus, one can safely say that there are scientific reasons behind wearing the janeyu.

The janeyu is worn on the left shoulder by an orthodox Hindu. It has six holy threads for a married man and three for a *brahmachari* or bachelor. In the south, old janeyus are discarded and new ones are worn on the shravana purnima, while chanting the Gayatri Mantra. Similarly, following a birth or death in the family, the janeyu is removed and replaced with a new one after thirteen days of the event. This is done because the janeyu is not an ordinary thread; its sanctity is liable to be disturbed if it is not worn properly or changed on occurrence of some inauspicious event.

Similar to Hindus, Parsis too wear the *kusti* around their waist, which symbolizes the tenets of their faith. A kusti is woven with seventy-two threads of fine lambs' wool. The number of threads denotes the chapters in the *Yasna*, the Parsi book of worship.

33

Why Is the *Shankha* Sacred in Hinduism?

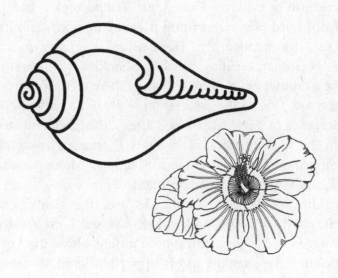

Mythology and Legends

The sacred shell or conch is known as shankha in Sanskrit. A sacred and religious object in Hinduism, the sound of the shankha symbolizes the divine sound of Aum. It derives its name from the demon Shankha asura, whom Lord Vishnu had slain as *matsya* avatar or fish incarnation by blowing Aum into the conch-shaped bone of the asura's ear.

The *Brahma Vaivarta Purana* tells us about the creation of conches. Once Lord Vishnu took a trident from Lord Shiva and flung it at the demons, burning them instantaneously. Their ashes flew over to the Ksheersagar, creating conches. Shankha is believed to be a brother of Lakshmi as both of them were born from the sea. Due to the association of shankha with water, serpents or nagas are named after it. Nagas mentioned in the Mahabharata, *Harivamsha Purana* and *Bhagavat Purana* include names like Shankha, Mahashankha, Shankhapala and Shankhachuda.

Brahma Vaivarta Purana declares the shankha as the abode of both Goddess Lakshmi and Lord Vishnu. Images of Vishnu, sitting or standing, show the Lord holding the shankha in his upper left hand, denoting dharma or righteousness.

This sacred object is closely associated with Vishnu. Vishnu's avatars, such as the matsya, *kurma*, *varaha* and *narasimha* are depicted holding the shankha along with other symbols of Vishnu. Regional forms of Vishnu like Lord Jagannath at Puri, in Orissa; Lord Venkatesh at Balaji, in Andhra Pradesh; and Lord Vithoba in

Pandharpur, in Maharashtra are also pictured holding a shankha. Sometimes, Vishnu's shankha is personified as *ayudha purush*. Similarly, Gaja Lakshmi idols show the goddess holding a shankha in her right hand.

In the Ramayana, Lakshmana, Bharata and Shatrughna are considered part incarnations of Sheshanaga, Sudarshana Chakra and Shankha, respectively.

During the war at Kurukshetra, between the Pandavas and the Kauravas, Krishna, as the charioteer of Arjuna, blew his conch, the Panchajanya — which means having control over five classes of beings — to declare the beginning of the epic war. All the Pandava brothers had their own shankhas — Yudhishtira's was called Ananta Vijaya; Bhima's was called Poundra Khadga; Arjuna's was Devadatta; Nakula's was Sughosha; and Sahadeva's was Mani Pushpaka.

The shankha has different regional names. In Sanskrit, Kannada, Marathi and Hindi, it is called shankha. In Gujarati, it is known as *da-sukh*, *chanku* in Tamil, *soukham* in Telugu and *shaankh* in Bengali.

Types of Shankhas

A shankha, in fact, is the shell of a large predatory sea snail — *Turbinella pyrum* — found in Indian waters. However, in English, the shell of this species is known as the 'sacred conch' or the 'divine chank'.

Like all snail shells, the interior of this shell is hollow and very shiny. Based on the direction of coiling, shankhas have two varieties — the *vamavarti* and the *dakshinavarti*. The vamavarti shankha is commonly available and its coils or whorls expand in a clockwise spiral, whereas the dakshinavarti shankha is very rare. The coils or whorls of this expand counterclockwise. This is a very rarely formed shape and is considered auspicious and a giver of wealth. As per Hindu belief, the dakshinavarti shankha is like a rare jewel or *ratna*.

In Hinduism, a dakshinavarti shankha symbolizes infinite space. Even if such a shankha has a defect, mounting it with gold restores its merits. The *Skanda Purana* narrates that bathing Vishnu with a dakshinavarti shankha grants the devotee freedom from the sins of seven previous births. According to another belief, bathing a deity with the waters led through a shankha — preferably the dakshinavarti — is considered equal to bathing it with all the holy water of the seven seas or the seven holy rivers. The price of such a rare shankha runs into lakhs of rupees.

Significance

In its earliest references, the shankha is mentioned as a trumpet and it is in this form that it became an emblem of Vishnu. Simultaneously, it was used as a votive offering and as a charm to keep away the dangers of the sea. It was the earliest known sound-producing agent.

As a trumpet or wind instrument, a hole is drilled near the tip of the apex of the shankha. When air is blown through this hole, it travels through the whorls producing a loud, sharp and shrill sound. This particular quality of sound is the reason why shankha was used as a war trumpet, to summon helpers and friends. The shankha continued to be used in battles for a long time. The war sound it produced was called *shankhanad*.

In Hindu scriptures, the shankha is praised as a giver of fame, longevity, prosperity and the dispeller of sins. Its antiquity is traced to the early days of Indian history when it was blown to drive away evil spirits and demons.

In ancient days, people were properly trained in blowing the conch, as there are different notes for blowing the conch on different occasions. It was blown with a soothing note to welcome an honoured guest; with a high-pitched, shrill note to announce victory; while the note that emitted from the conch during arati was quite different. In Orissa, there is a community whose people can blow two conches at a time.

Ancient India lived mostly in villages. Each village was presided over by a principal temple and several small ones. During the arati of the deity, the conch would invariably be blown, as it is done even today. Since villages were generally small, the sound of the conch would resound all over the village. Those who could not make it to the temple or were not allowed in, would stop whatever they were doing for a few seconds and mentally bow to the Almighty. Thus, the sound of the conch served to elevate people's minds to a piety even in the middle of their busy daily routine. In Islam, this is achieved through the azan—the calling of the faithful to prayer.

It is popularly believed that a person who regularly blows a conch never develops any respiratory problem.

His lungs are never adversely affected. Listening to the sound of the conch is said to benefit those who are dumb or who stammer. By blowing the conch, one throws out the stale air present in the body and replaces it with fresh, revitalizing air.

The well-known scientist, Acharya Jagadish Chandra Bose, proved that by regularly blowing the conch and ringing bells, the immediate surroundings become pure and peaceful as its sound removes negativity from the area. That is why when we go to traditionally maintained temples, we find them serene and comforting.

Scientifically too, the blowing of conch has benefits. It is an established fact that the sun's rays obstruct the expansion of sound. For this reason, radio transmissions are less clear during the day than at night. Therefore, the conch is blown at holy places at about sunrise and near sunset. When a man blows the conch in the correct manner, its sound either destroys the bacteria in the atmosphere that is harmful to humans or makes them inactive. Thus, blowing the conch cleanses the surroundings.

Uses of the Shankha

Nowadays, the shankha is blown at the time of worship in Hindu temples and homes, especially during the arati, when light is offered to the deities. The shankha is also used to bathe images of deities, especially Vishnu, and for ritual purification. No hole is drilled into shankhas that are used for bathing purposes or for distributing *tirtham* or holy water.

After a puja, priests, especially in south India, distribute tirtham to devotees through a conch. The science behind this ritual is that the conch has sulphur, phosphorus and calcium; therefore, the water kept in such a vessel makes it medicinal. The puja enhances its divinity; hence the name of such water is tirtham. Moreover, when the conch water is sprinkled over people and objects, it disinfects them.

The shankha has several other uses. It is used as a material for making bangles, bracelets and other objects. Due to its aquatic origin and resemblance to the vulva, it has become an integral part of tantric rites. In view of this, its symbolism is also said to represent female fertility. It is mentioned that in ancient Greece, shells, along with pearls, denoted sexual love and marriage, and also the female energy, *adyashakti*.

The shankha is also used in Ayurvedic medicinal formulations to treat many ailments. Conch shell ash is known in Sanskrit as *shankhabhasma*. It is prepared by soaking the shell in lime juice and then calcining in covered crucibles ten to twelve times, and finally reducing it to powder. Shankhabhasma contains calcium, iron and magnesium and is considered to possess antacid and digestive properties.

Interestingly, the shankha was the royal state emblem of the erstwhile state of Travancore. Puri, in Orissa, is known as Shakkha-Kshetra. It is also the election symbol of the Indian political party, the Biju Janata Dal.

34

Why Do Hindus Match Horoscopes before Fixing a Marriage?

The *Markandeya Purana* states that for a healthy and proper family life, people must marry. The modern concept of living-in may find favour at the individual level, but where society is concerned, it is undesirable. According to Hindu belief and thought, marriage is a social and formal commitment to respect, care for, and take the responsibility of one's spouse. It has a purpose, a duty towards one's family to continue its progeny, a social obligation to abide by the norms of society, and to carry forward values and traditions of our culture. With marriage comes sensual love in one's life. It also gives a family of one's own. Therefore, one must choose one's life partner with thoughtful consideration.

When horoscopes of a prospective bride and groom are matched, a number of considerations are deliberated upon, such as whether or not the union of the two will be mutually satisfying, the couple will bear children, the marriage will last long, the couple will be socially, intellectually and sexually compatible and so on.

According to ancient scriptures, human nature is categorized in three categories; godly or *devagana*, devilish or *rakshasagana*, and humanly or *naragana*. The horoscope of an individual reflects this aspect of the individual's character in its charts. While matching two horoscopes, it is usually ensured that a rakshasagana man does not marry a naragana woman because in such a case, the man will not sacrifice his egos and, therefore, will not keep the woman emotionally happy. He will tend to dominate her throughout their married life. On the contrary, when a naragana woman marries a devagana or naragana man, or manusha gana, she will be happy in marriage. By matching horoscopes, one can avoid undesirable unions. Moreover, marriage is a commitment where both partners have to sacrifice their egos for conjugal harmony. Matching horoscopes helps in understanding whether they will sacrifice their egos for each other or not. However, the results of matching birth charts will only be true if the horoscopes have been accurately cast. In case these are inaccurate, the predictions will not come true and matching of horoscopes will have no meaning.

Through marriage, a couple seeks physical pleasure also. Therefore, the sex life of a couple is also considered while matching horoscopes. Will the marriage offer a sexually satisfying life for both, will the couple bear children in a timely manner, will children born of the marriage be healthy? Such aspects of marriage are taken into account while matching birth charts. Marriages within the same *gotra*, or lineage, are prohibited. The science behind this taboo is that siblings born of such a marriage are likely to be unhealthy or physically challenged. Germans have carried out research on this subject that has endorsed this view. The ill effects of such a marriage may not be evident instantly, but will certainly show up on a later day. Modern men, however, do not believe in such social taboos. Incidentally, while the Hindu Act does not restrict marriages in the same gotra, traditional Hindu law does not approve of such marriages.

In the case of love marriages, it is often observed that relations between a couple before marriage are sweet and cordial, but after marriage they gradually become sour and bitter. This happens because, perhaps, according to their birth charts, these two people can be good friends but may not necessarily be good life partners.

Another important aspect of married life, evaluated at the time of tallying birth charts, is the span of married life. A good astrologer can predict the longevity of a marriage. The mental compatibility of the two is also calculated at the time of matching the horoscopes. Difference of more than 5 per cent in the mental level is undesirable for a happy married life, as per the scriptures. The mahurat or time of solemnizing the marriage is also determined, for best results.

These are some of the reasons why horoscopes are tallied before a marriage alliance is finalized. The only prerequisite is that the birth charts have to be accurate; else the predictions will be incorrect. Modern man, however, is indifferent to such beliefs. He does not feel the need to consult any astrologer before forming an alliance. To some extent, he is right because these days, one hardly finds an astrologer worth the name. Moreover, there is no guarantee for the accuracy of birth charts which is a must for matching horoscopes for prefect results. In such situations, results are bound to be erratic and uncertain.

35

What Is the Significance of a *Mangalsutra* and Kumkum for a Married Hindu Woman?

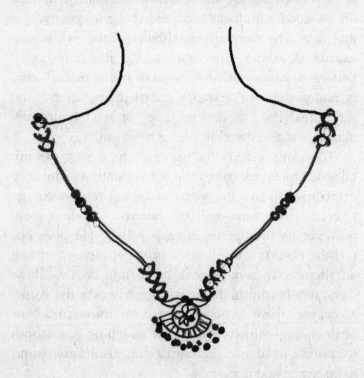

In the Hindu tradition, marriage is a holy alliance between two souls. There is a purpose behind it and a sense of duty towards one's family to continue the progeny together with a social obligation to abide by its laws, norms, values and traditions. A marriage founded on such high values is bound to be happy, harmonious and progressive.

During the formative days of ancient Hindu society, rishis and munis formed and developed the institution of marriage after great deliberations. Through their past experiences, wise Indian men realized that for a happy marriage, the two partners have to be sincere, loyal and caring. They also realized that as a mother, wife and daughter, the woman plays a major role in keeping different relations intact in a family.

Sage Shwetaketu, a great social thinker in the early years of Vedic society, worked out details for the institution of marriage which were later amended and improved. He laid down the guidelines, norms, chronology of rituals, customs and traditions related to marriage.

The principal purpose of his framing marriage customs and traditions was to ensure lasting harmony in relations not only between the two people directly involved but also between the two families. While laying down details, sage Shwetaketu kept in mind the psychological, physical and mental needs of the couple so that they bond well with each other, and for life. He decided on such customs and traditions that served as lifelong reminders of sincerity and loyalty—the most important aspects of a successful marriage.

The most significant change the wise sage introduced was to give the maiden a new identity at the time of her marriage. Apart from the mangalsutra—*mangal* means 'well-being' and *sutra* means 'thread'; it is worn for the well-being of the husband—toe rings, kumkum, bangles and nose ring were made mandatory for a woman for her married life. These five sacred symbols gave the woman a distinct identity and responsibility. Of the five symbols, the mangalsutra enjoys a greater degree of sanctity, being an ornament of sacred bondage.

Mangalsutra literally means an auspicious thread. Originally, it was just a gold pendant strung from a yellow thread prepared with turmeric paste, together with a string of black beads, called *manjari*. The mangalsutra is tied around the neck of the bride on the day of marriage, symbolizing the union. Though it is comparable to the wedding ring of the West, it has a greater significance.

In north India and in the Marathi–Konkani regions, this ornament is called the mangalsutra, but in Tamil, Telegu and Malayalam cultures, it is referred to as *thali*.

A married woman is expected to wear the mangalsutra until her husband's death. According to tradition, the families of the bride and the bridegroom both contribute a piece of gold and melt them together with the help of the family goldsmith. This is then used to make the rest of the necklace. However, these days, mangalsutras are available off the shelf and are not made as per tradition.

The mangalsutra is made in numerous designs. The more popular ones are the *ramarpottu* thali, worn by Telugus and Kannadigas; *ela* thali, worn by the Malayalis; and *kumbha* thali, worn by the Tamils of the Kshatriya caste. The design is chosen by the groom's family, according to prevalent customs. Gujaratis and Marwaris often use a diamond pendant. Maharashtrians wear a pendant of one or two *vati*s. Bengali, Odiya and Assamese people don't have the custom of wearing the mangalsutra.

According to the Hindu cultural ethos, the mangalsutra symbolizes the inseparable bond between a husband and a wife. During the wedding ceremony, the bridegroom ties the mangalsutra around the neck of the bride, with three knots. He utters, 'May you live long by wearing this sacred mangalsutra,' during a ceremony called *mangalya dharanam*, while the priests recite Vedic hymns and mantras. In some customs, the groom ties the first knot and his sister ties the other two knots. Later, the mangalsutra may be restrung on some auspicious day in the form of a necklace made of gold and black beads on one or two yellow threads or gold chains with an elaborate pendant of gold or diamond. Each black bead in the mangalsutra is believed to have divine powers that protect the married couple from the evil eye, and is believed to safeguard the life of the husband. Most Hindu women are extremely superstitious about the mangalsutra. If it breaks or gets lost, it is considered ominous. Therefore, the mangalsutra is much more than a piece of jewellery: it is a sacred necklace of love, trust and marital happiness — a vital symbol of wedlock. Married women are entitled to wear the mangalsutra throughout their lives as it is believed to enhance the well-being of the husband and family.

With changing times, especially in the metros, for women who are not stay-at-home wives, the concept of wearing a mangalsutra has changed visibly. Now, it is more of a fashion statement than a symbol of marriage.

The ancient wise men of India devised the mangalsutra for the well-being of the couple and their married life. How the modern-day woman looks at this amulet will depend on her personal perception, and the constraints of the jet age.

Why Do Married Women Apply Kumkum?

One of the symbols of an orthodox Hindu married woman is the application of *sindoor*, the vermilion powder, in the parting of her hair, and sporting a *bindi* or a dot of kumkum in the centre of her forehead, between the two eyebrows.

Pure kumkum is obtained with unadulterated turmeric powder mixed with filtered lime water or lemon juice and camphor. The desired result of kumkum will only be achieved when it is pure and is prepared as per tradition. Kumkum that is currently available in the market cannot create the intended effect as it is made with chemical dyes. Pure kumkum is prepared with great care and faith, chanting mantras all the while.

Turmeric is grown underground; hence it has the elements, properties and qualities of earth in it. *Dharti* or Mother Earth is the personification of tolerance. Since turmeric is obtained from earth, it naturally has the power of absorption and tolerance. When lime water or lemon juice is added to it, it turns red which denotes action or activity.

Applying pure kumkum on the forehead between the two eyebrows, where the centre of thoughts — the ajna chakra — is located, gives a woman strength to bear the additional responsibilities of household after marriage. For the first time, the husband applies the kumkum in his bride's hair parting during the marriage ceremony, thereby symbolizing that she would henceforth be a *grihastha* or householder with additional responsibilities of a wife. It also denotes her marital status — a tradition that is unique to Indian culture.

Using present day plastic, reusable bindis, or kumkum made of chemicals, does not create the intended effect. It may, however, serve the cosmetic purpose.

36

Why Do Hindus Cremate
Their Dead?

Hindus usually dispose of their dead by cremating them. They hold the view that by burning the dead, the human body disintegrates faster into its basic five elements, the panchabhootas, when compared with other methods of disposing the dead. Also, the bacteria get burnt along with the body of the deceased. However, an infant up to the age of fourteen months is either buried or given *jal pravaha* or immersion into water. A unique feature of cremation is that Hindus carry out kapal kriya during the rite: the person performing the last rites opens up the burning skull with a bamboo to release the remaining locked prana or life in the brain of the deceased, thereby ensuring a quick disintegration into the panchabhootas.

The Manikarnika Ghat at Varanasi is a world renowned cremation ground that receives sixty to 100 dead bodies each day for cremation. It is said that the ghat has been in existence since the time of King Harishchandra of the Puranic days. To perform the last rites at this ghat, one is expected to take the eternal fire from the kund or fireplace, which, according to legend, has never been put out in thousands of years. No matchstick is used to light the fire at Manikarnika. The cremation ground at Delhi, the Nigam Bodh Ghat, on the banks of river Yamuna, is equally old, dating back to the times of the Mahabharata.

Strangely, the people of the Indus Valley buried their dead, as is evident from excavations at different sites belonging to that period. In fact, the very name Mohenjo-Daro literally means 'the mound of the dead'. At a later date, they realized that burial of the dead covered substantial land which could otherwise be utilized for society. Cremation, on the other hand, needed just a piece of land for disposal of the dead.

Some unorthodox and non-traditional Hindus nowadays take their dead to an electric crematorium in cosmopolitan cities. Of late, some people in the West are reportedly preferring cremation to burial; the trend is on the increase in the US and Europe.

There are a few more scientific practices associated with death in an orthodox Hindu family. In the olden days, people attending to a dying person would immediately remove him from the bed when they realized that he was about to breath his last. The body would be placed on the floor or ground, with his feet towards the south. The science behind this practice was simple and clear. When a man dies, the life force or vital energy — a subtle electrical discharge — leaves the body and he dies peacefully. Since the floor or ground is a good conductor of electricity, placing the body thus helps the vital energy to leave the body quickly and the man dies with no or little discomfort. In the past, beds and cots were made of wood and bamboo, both of which were bad conductors of electricity. Subsequently, when allowed to remain on the bed or cot, the dying person would face a great deal of anxiety and difficulty as the release of vital force from his body would get delayed. The body was placed with its feet towards the south so that the polar gravitational pull works on it and eases the quick and smooth release of vital energy from the dying person.

Another practice prevalent in orthodox families is that after cremation of the dead and before leaving the cremation ground, the mourners are supposed to chew a few leaves of the neem tree for a while and then spit these out. This is done to disinfect the mouth which is prone to be infected at a cremation ground. Similarly, in rural India, the house where a member has died is plastered afresh with a paste of cow dung, a disinfectant. Modern scientists confirm this fact. Such rites and rituals as prevalent in Hindu society indeed have scientific backing.

37

Why Do Hindus Observe Fasts?

The dictionary meaning of the word 'fast' is to 'abstain from eating' or 'go without food'. In the traditional sense, 'fast' has a different connotation. In Sanskrit, fasting is called *upavas*. *Upa* means 'near' and *vas* means 'to stay'. Upavas, therefore, means to stay near God. In other words, it refers to a mental state wherein a man lives in close proximity with the Almighty. When a man observes upavas, he spends the day mostly by reciting God's names and offering his service at holy places such as temples or ashrams.

People observe fasts to gain spiritual strength and health. When fasting, most Indians eat once a day or make do only with fruit or simple, light food; some do not eat at all. Abstaining from food rests both the digestive system and the entire body. Fasting helps us gain control over our senses and our craving for food. It steers our mind to be poised and at peace. On the day of Shivaratri, while on fast, we should think of Lord Shiva throughout the day. Similarly, on Krishnastmi, we should sing songs in praise of Krishna till midnight; and during navaratri fasts, we should devote ourselves to Ma Durga.

Hindu scriptures prescribe only satvik food during fasts. Besides satvik food—products of milk, and food with less spices—a special diet that finds favour with a particular deity is also prescribed. For instance, when you observe a fast to appease Saturn, you should eat food consisting of black gram, jaggery and linseeds, because these items are in harmony with saturn. Likewise, when you undertake a fast to please the sun god Surya, you should eat saltless food because salt is not in harmony with Surya. Prescriptions or restrictions about diet have been laid down by our rishis and munis after in-depth study of all the planets and other astral bodies. To receive best results of your *vrat* food, you must meditate on your meal, observe silence, and eat slowly.

An interesting scientific fact about the ekadashi vrat—fast on the eleventh lunar day of each fortnight of the month—is that on this day, bile juices collected by our digestive system during the previous ten days are distributed to various parts and organs of our body to strengthen them. In order to enable our body system to properly distribute these bile juices, seers and saints advised us to observe this fast. This was devised by them after studying the cycle of the human biological system. Modern-day scientists and doctors are yet to make such a detailed study of the human body.

The Bhagavad Gita urges us to eat neither too less nor too much, i.e., *yukta ahara*, even while not fasting. Sadly, the modern man indulges in overeating even on days that he observes a fast. During Navaratris, certain popular chains of restaurant are seen commercializing food for people observing fasts. In the name of 'fasting food', these branded food outlets provide high-calorie fried food. The whole idea of observing a fast is completely defeated if 'fasting food' is turned to 'feasting food'.

While Hindus observe fasts on various days and festivals, Jains have a special period of ten days in the month of bhadra (August–September) when they observe fast. The uniqueness of this fast is that they do not consume anything except water. Some devout Jains do not even take water. During the month of Ramadan, Muslims too observe *roza*s or fasts. Most Muslims do not consume anything after sunrise and before sunset during this month. Jews and Parsis have their own days for observing fasts. Whatever be the religious reasons, the fact remains that fasting completely overhauls the urinary, circulatory, digestive and respiratory systems.

38

Why Do Hindus Believe in Giving Charity?

Charity and compassion have been the two pillars of Indian culture through ages. The concept of *dana* or charity is probably the oldest religious concept propagated in ancient India. One of the hymns of the tenth canto of the Rig Veda states: 'Wealth of a person never diminishes by charity; nobody helps one who fails to be charitable.' To give without asking is the attribute of God, who gives light to all through the sun, provides water to sustain life through rivers, and the vital air to breath. When a man practises charity, his behaviour and attitude are likened to that of God. In return, nature rewards a man by compensating tenfold for his beneficent acts. According to divine design, if you give something to nature, you will be repaid manifold.

The Gita follows the Upanishads in upholding the virtues of charity. It speaks of three kinds of charities: satvik, rajasik and tamasik. Satvik charity is that which is given out of a sense of social duty, without any expectation of repayment of any kind. Rajasik charity is that which is given as a repayment of certain obligations, and with the desire of begetting some result out of the charitable act. And tamasik charity is one which is given to someone insultingly. *Dharmashastra*s differ considerably about the amount one should spend on charity out of his income.

Giving food and water is considered the highest form of charity by the scriptures. The Mahabharata enjoins people to build water reservoirs and dig wells. These acts are considered as great social charity. Planting trees is also considered an altruistic act. The epic advises that man should nurture trees as if they were his own sons. The 'Shanti Parva' of the Mahabharata prohibits the householder from enjoying the fruits of his labour and wealth all alone. In the past, people built *dharamshalas* or free guest houses, orphanages and temples as great acts of dana. In ancient religious texts, certain days were prescribed when acts of charity were mandatory. For instance, on the day of *nirjala* ekadashi, people offer water or sherbet to passers-by. Similarly, on the day of an eclipse, Hindus offer grains, salt and money to the underprivileged. When people go to pilgrimages, they readily involve themselves in acts of charity. But wealth or money for charity must be earned through honest ways; otherwise the donation will bear no result, thus states the *Garuda Purana*. Another important instruction about giving donations is that they should only be given to genuinely needy and deserving people.

Feeding animals, birds, insects and watering plants and trees are also considered a form of donation. These activities heal our karmas and help take away some of our problems. When these life forms share our food, kitchen and water resources, they in return share our sorrows too, and thus reduce our karmic debts.

Modern man has also realized the pleasure of giving and is seen celebrating 'Joy of Giving Week' and giving donations and gifts to the less privileged. Organ donation is a modern act of charity. Donation to the Prime Minister's Relief Fund during national calamities is another way of modern donation, though some do so to avail of income tax rebate.

Other religions also lay emphasis on charity. In Islam, *zakarat* or charity during the month of Ramadan is an act of great merit. Muslims are required to donate 2.5 per cent of their income. Christianity is equally vocal on charity.

39

Why Do Hindus Believe in Rising Early in the Morning?

Modern scientists accept that all human thoughts have electromagnetic energy. And energy can never be destroyed; it can be manifested in a different form. Every day, after sunset, nature releases thought energy into the astral world. This released thought energy goes up and returns daily to earth, duly charged with astral energy between about 3 a.m. and 4 a.m. This divine hour in the Hindu scriptures has been defined as *brahma muhurta*. Those who are awake during this auspicious hour receive the transformed energy and realize their desires.

However, for anyone to realize his desires, the sincerity, purity and intensity of his thoughts are of great importance. The more intense and sincere the desire, the higher it goes up into the astral world and returns accordingly charged with divine force. This is the spiritual explanation of the phenomenon that Indian yogis, seers and saints realized thousands of years ago.

There is yet another explanation for waking up early in the morning. During the night, trees and plants release oxygen into the atmosphere, which is so very vital for human health. One who gets up early and performs his chores receives fresh, revitalizing air and benefits himself.

These two scientific facts amply explain the truth behind the old saying: 'Early to bed and early to rise, makes a man healthy, wealthy and wise.'

40

Why Do Hindus Prostrate at the Feet of Their Parents, Teachers and Holy Men?

Most people of the world have one or two accepted norms of salutation and greeting. However, Hindus have a great variety in this. Conventionally, Indians prostrate at the feet of their parents, elders, teachers and holy souls and touch their feet. The gesture is known as *pranam* or prostration. Elders, in turn, bless us by placing their hand on or over our heads. In traditional homes, pranam is done daily when we meet elders for the first time each day and also on occasions like birthdays, festivals, after performing pujas, and while starting a new venture, to receive their blessings.

According to Hindu thought, every man has two sources of light in his body, which can be seen by a spiritually advanced soul such as a yogi or a mahatma. Of the two sources of light, one is *akash* or ether which is a magnetic energy that outlines our body. The other is *shree* or the aura which emits light in a circular fashion, around one's head, from the Brahma *talu* or the top of the head. In common language, this light is referred to as the 'halo of a person'. This halo varies from person to person, depending upon his spiritual level.

In the gesture of bowing down, one touches one's elders' or parents' feet, more specifically, the *varishtha angushtha* or the big toe of the feet where we find the longest nerve that connects to the Brahma talu. The aura radiates like a fountain of light from this point of the body. Through the process of *ashirwad*, elders, parents, gurus and saints transfer their energy in a mystical manner by touching the Brahma talu of the one seeking the ashirwad. The entire process will be well understood if we further analyse the posture of pranam.

When someone is offering pranam to his guru or parents, he bends down to touch their toes, and they reciprocate by touching his Brahma talu; thus a cycle of energy is created that unites the two bodies with cosmic energy. In other words, the guru's energy is channelized from his blessing hands to the body of the seeker who receives it by touching the guru's toes.

Pranam and *namaskar* are, in fact, different ways of spiritual *mudra*s or postures meant for saluting gods and spiritual people. Generally, there are six kinds of pranams.

The first one is called the *sashtanga* or eight-limb pranaam, in which a devout prostrates and eight parts of the seeker's body touch the ground — knees, stomach, chest, chin, nose, temple, hands and elbows. In this gesture, the devout also swings his head thrice to touch the ground with both his temples and the forehead. This pranam is offered to holy men and saints.

However, the most common type of pranam is the *shadanga* or six limb pranam, in which six parts of the seeker's body touch the ground — knees, toes, hands, stomach, nose and forehead. This pranam is generally offered to deities in temples. There is yet another pranam called the *panchanga* or five-limb pranam in which five portions of the body are lowered — toes, knees, hands, nose and forehead. While prostrating, we touch the earth, which is an effective yogic practice that helps us to return to our basic self.

The fourth posture is the *dandavata* pranam in which a devout merely bows his forehead to the ground and touches the toes of the guru and elders to receive their blessings, which they give by touching his Brahma talu.

The fifth is namaskar, which means *namah* — I bow to you. Namaskar is touching the forehead with the thumbs of your folded hands thrice. Touching the forehead where the frontal lobe of the brain is placed symbolically means that one is knocking at the eternal vision or the point of the third eye. This is also that part of the body which manipulates the higher mental functions of a person.

The sixth kind of salutation is known as *abhinandan* or welcome in which the person gently bends his head forward with folded hands, touching one's own chest, thereby saying that 'you reside in my heart' or 'you are dear to me'. Air hostesses welcome us aboard planes by the abhinandan greeting.

41

What Is the Significance of *Namaste*?

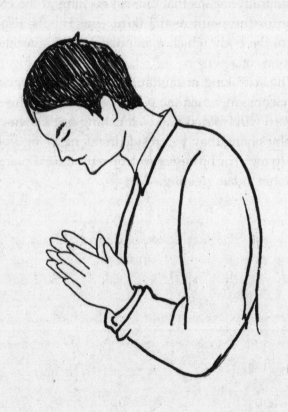

Indians generally greet each other by saying namaste. While doing so, the two palms are placed together in front of the chest, with a slightly bowed head. This greeting is for all — for people older or younger to us, for friends, and even for strangers.

In Sanskrit, when namah is combined with *te*, we get 'namaste', which means 'I bow to you' or 'my greetings and salutations to you'. 'Namah' can literally be interpreted as 'na-ma' or 'not me' — I have no ego before you. This also has a social significance. By negating or subduing one's ego in the presence of another, we generate goodwill in our relations. The bowing down of the head is a gracious form of extending friendship with love and humility. When we say 'namaste' with humility and respect, we invoke good wishes and blessings of elders.

The spiritual import of saying 'namaste' is even deeper. The life force, the Divine, the self, or the Lord in me is the same as in all others. Recognizing divinity in all, we say 'namaste' with a bowed head and folded palms; in other words, we bow to the divinity in the person we meet, regardless of his caste, colour or creed. Thus, 'namaste', if sincerely said, spreads universal love.

42

Why Is It Considered Improper to Step on Top of Books and Other Educational Objects?

Virtues and knowledge were highly regarded in ancient India. A man was adjudged not by his wealth, but by his knowledge. The great rishis and munis of the past held knowledge as sacred and divine. Therefore, it must be accorded respect at all times. In the olden days, every subject—academic or spiritual— was considered holy, and was taught by gurus in open schools known as *gurukul*s.

The tradition of not stepping on books and other educational tools, even inadvertently, is a reminder of the elevated position accorded to knowledge in Indian culture. Psychologically, this attitude towards books fosters in us, from an early age, a deep reverence for books and educational objects.

There are other reasons as well for not stepping upon books. Socially, stepping on books is equivalent to disrespecting and disregarding them. Scientifically speaking, a man discharges negativity through his feet; therefore, when we step on books and other such educational tools, we make them unholy. And when we read such unholy books, we do not receive the required and desired vibrations from them.

In the Hindu calendar, a day is marked to respect and worship our books. On the day of Basant Panchami, in the month of February every year, Hindus worship their books, pens, and ink, and perform Saraswati Puja to honour the goddess of learning—Saraswati.

Not only on books, stepping upon a human being is also considered a sin in Hindu thoughts. Man is the crown creation of nature. He is regarded as the most beautiful and living temple of the Supreme Lord. Therefore, touching another person with our feet or stepping upon him is akin to disrespecting the divinity within him. Such an act calls for an immediate apology, and should be offered with reverence and humility by the offender.

43

Why Is It Essential for Hindus to Have a Prayer Room in Their Homes?

In Hindu thought, all that exists in this universe belongs to the Supreme Lord. He is the architect of the entire design. Therefore, most traditional Indian homes have a prayer room. The intent behind this is to acknowledge that the Lord is the real owner of our house, we are simply the earthly occupants of his property. Such a notion rids us of false pride and possessiveness.

In the prayer room, we light a lamp each day to remember and worship the Almighty, or our deity. Other spiritual practices such as japa, the repetition of the Almighty's name, meditation, reading of holy scriptures, prayers and devotional singing are also done here, including special pujas on auspicious and festive days. Each member of the family, young or old, communes with and worships the Divine in this room or space. All these sincere activities purify and divinize the place. When one enters such a charged room, one feels peaceful and solaced. The divine vibrations— created by lighting lamp with pure ghee from cow milk, burning aromatic incense, grounding sandalwood and offering fresh flowers—spread to other rooms of the house. Such houses turn into personal temples, and when an outsider visits the house, he too feels happy and peaceful.

The ideal attitude is to regard the Supreme Being as the true owner of our home and consider ourselves as his caretaker. Should you find it difficult to accept this concept, at least think of him as a welcome guest during the puja hours and treat him thus. We must keep the prayer room clean and well decorated. As the saying goes, cleanliness is next to godliness.

Scientifically, participation in holy activities and meditating in the puja room fills the entire house with good vibrations and charges it with positive energy. Families living in such homes normally do not break up; they neither experience want of money nor do they indulge in unpleasant, loud arguments as the Almighty's grace pervades all over the house. All tasks undertaken by the incumbents of such homes are successful and accomplished. It is for these reasons that we should have a separate room or least at a corner as the prayer room or area.

44

Why Do Hindus Believe in the Gotra System?

In Vedic Sanskrit, the word 'gotra' means 'cowshed'. However, in the social context, it refers to the lineage of clan assigned to a Hindu at birth. As most traditions of the Hindu system are patrilineal, the gotra of one's father is assigned to the newly born. In some communities in south India, such as among the Nairs of Kerala, the gotra is passed through the mother. In Vedic society, gotra was initially used by the Sanatana, the ancient-most people for identification of the lineage. In traditional Hindu families, gotra is important while fixing marriages as marriages cannot take place within the same gotra because this may affect the health of the progeny. These are prohibited under the rule of exogamy in the traditional system. People within the same gotra are regarded as kin, therefore marrying a kin would be thought of as incest.

Before proceeding further, it is necessary to distinguish gotra from *kula*. A kula is a set of people following similar cultural practices, often worshipping the same divinity—the kula devata or devi, the god or goddess of the clan—and following the same rituals, but they need not belong to the same lineage. Therefore, marriage within the kula was allowed; rather, it was preferred in ancient society.

Traditionally, Brahmanical gotras relate directly to the original seven *mula purusha* or the *saptarshis*— Pulastya, Pulaha, Kratu, Atri, Angiras, Vashishtha and Marichi. With time, the concept of gotra was extended beyond Brahmins. In other words, in the Sanatana society, there were only seven gotras but later, their number increased and more gotras were added after the name of other mula purushas who were not Brahmins. Other terms synonymous with gotra are *vamsha*, *vamshaja*, *purvajana* and *pitri*. In the present-day Hindu system, gotra is applied to all the lineage systems. In fact, many modern Hindus have lineages that do not follow the Vedic classification.

The modern generation is unmindful of this tradition and looks upon it as an outdated concept. According to a German study, marriages outside one's gotra are healthier and desirable on account of better genetic mutation. This anatomical fact was well realized by the ancient rishis and they forbade marriage within seven generations of the same gotra because genetic impacts can be seen up to seven generations. Modern man and medical science must undertake research on this subject to discover the truth of this age-old belief. So many modern-day diseases that have appeared in the last four decades may give geneticists an insight into the veracity of this old system. The adverse effects of such marriages may not be immediately evident but, over a period of time, they certainly show up in the offspring. These days, the purity of line is very hard to maintain because of prevalent lifestyles and liberal sexual practices. Therefore, gotra has become more or less irrelevant.

Marriages within the same gotra are, however, legal, though traditional social set-ups, particularly in Uttar Pradesh, Rajasthan and Haryana often agitate over them. The *khap* panchayats, the self-styled village courts, should recognize marriages within the same gotra as legal and hence, should be socially accepted. Those who oppose *sagotra*—belonging to the same lineage or gotra—marriages must realize that ancient wisdom is valid only when the parents' own lineage is pure and uncorrupted. The same cannot be claimed in present-day society and, therefore, their argument is not valid.

The growing demand of khap panchayats to amend the Hindu Marriage Act to disallow same-gotra marriages under the garb of science—that marriages within a family or clan can result in genetic defects in the offspring—is unjustified because the Hindu society has since undergone radical changes; the lineage system is broken and the purity of the progeny or lineage is lost.

The Bombay High Court had settled the issue in 1945, declaring that marriage between two consenting individuals of the same gotra is not prohibited and that law does not bar such a relationship. Two reputed judges went into the issue sixty-five years ago after lengthy discussions with leading experts and investigations into the wisdom of the Hindu scriptures to arrive at their verdict. The case in question was *Madhavrao* vs *Raghavendrarao*, which involved a Deshastha Brahmin couple. The two-judge bench included Harilal J. Kania, the first Chief Justice of independent India, and P.B. Gajendragadkar, who became the Chief Justice of India in 1964.

Following a series of hearings, the bench came to the conclusion that a matrimonial alliance between a man and a woman belonging to same gotra was valid. The court clarified that there was a need for society to modify the tradition of denouncing such marriages to keep up with the changing times. It said, 'Courts have to construe the texts of Hindu law in the light of the explanations given by recognized commentators. But it must always be remembered that since the said commentaries were written, several centuries have passed by and during this long period, the Hindu mode of life has not remained still or static. Notions of good social behaviour and the general ideology of the Hindu society have been changing. The custom as to marriages between persons of the same gotra in this case is an eloquent instance in point.'

45

What Is the Wisdom behind Eating Food with Hands?

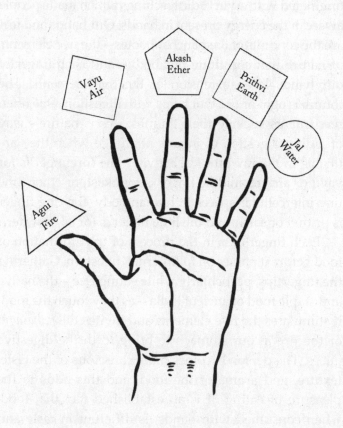

The West considers eating food with one's hands to be unhygienic, ill-mannered and primitive. However, since ancient times, Indians have believed that eating food with the hands feeds not only the body but also the mind and the soul.

The origin behind this old adage dates back to Vedic days when people ate with their hands. This practice originated with Ayurvedic teachings which made people aware of the energy present in hands. Our hands and feet are the conduits of the panchabhootas—the five elements of nature that constitute our body—and each finger of our hands is an extension of the five elements. The thumb is agni or fire that helps with digestion. One often sees infants sucking their thumbs; this is nature's way of aiding digestion of infants at an age when they are unable to do any physical activity. The forefinger is for vayu or air; the middle finger is for akash or ether—the tiny intercellular spaces in human body; the ring finger is prithvi or earth; and the little finger is for jal or water.

Each finger aids in the process of transformation of food before it passes on for internal digestion. Gathering the fingertips, particularly while eating rice—the native and staple food of ancient India—as they touch the food, it stimulates the five elements and invites the *jatharagni* or the fire in our stomach to bring forth the digestive juices. The person becomes more conscious of the taste, texture, and aroma of the food, and this adds to the pleasure of eating. It is an established fact that food, when consumed with hands, is different in taste and more palatable than food eaten with a fork and knife.

MISCELLANEOUS

46

'Aum' Is Eternal

'Aum' is divine: it is said to be the primordial monosyllabic sound that existed at the time of creation of the universe. It contains all other sounds, words, languages and mantras. Aum was born before anything else was born on earth. Before creation began, there was *Shunyakasha*—the emptiness or the void. Shunyakasha, literally meaning 'no sky', is actually more than nothingness; because everything then existed in a latent, potential state. The vibration of Aum symbolizes the manifestation of God in form. Aum is the reflection of the absolute reality; it is said to be *anadi*, *ananta*—without beginning or end—embracing all that exists.

In Sanskrit , Aum is known as the *pranava*, derived from the root *nu*, meaning 'to shout sound'. Therefore, *pra-nu* means to create a humming sound in your mind. It is also the symbol of the *sadi* Brahman, the Creator. It is believed that the sound that echoed and vibrated at the time of creation resembled Aum, and hence, it is accordingly pronounced.

Rhythm and harmony are intrinsic to nature. To align ourselves with the cosmos, we must be in sync with this rhythm. An important tool for this is to chant Aum, which has a unique sound that vibrates into the cosmos and penetrates deep within our psyche. The power of Aum is such that all inner illusions are dispelled and all negativity melts away. This sacred syllable emanates nectar from its very sound, and encompasses the past, present and future of the whole universe—it is beyond the periphery of Kaal or Time. Of the countless names of God, Aum is the most powerful. Aum is beyond all explanations; it is divine and above all the spheres of this physical world. In fact, all the sounds of the universe are born from it. The syllable of Aum cannot be governed by the rules of grammar; it is above all such rules.

The Big Bang theory also propounds similar thoughts: that the universe was created with a gigantic sound. Aum is universal in essence, without attributes of space and time. It is said that Lord Brahma started the creation of the world after chanting Aum. Hence, its sound is considered auspicious for beginning any new task; it creates favourable vibes and the task is accomplished.

The Gita expounds upon the chants *Aum-tat-sat*. At two instances in the holy book, Krishna says, 'I am Aum'. The Upanishads and Patanjali's *Yoga Sutra* have dwelt upon the spiritual, psychological and material benefits that accrue from sustained chanting of Aum— if done with full concentration. When chanted properly, it creates a highly charged field around the chanter, regardless of his faith, and elevates his spiritual level. It leaves a profound effect on the body and mind of the chanter as well as on the surroundings.

A natural question that emerges is: what is the proper way to chant this mystic syllable? Yogis have thus described the correct way of chanting Aum:

Take a deep breath, hold it for a while and then release it gradually, starting from the well of your navel and passing it through all the intermittent chakras between the navel and the throat. Continue breathing it out. However, before fully exhausting your breath, close your lips to allow the remaining breath to hum in the region of your mind.

By chanting Aum in this way, one's energy centres become activated and one benefits both spiritually and materialistically.

Aum is not just a sound or a vibration. Nor is it simply a symbol. It is the entire cosmos—everything that we can see, touch, hear, smell and feel. Moreover, it is all that is within our perception and all that is beyond it. It is the core of our very existence. To think of Aum only as a sound, a technique, or a symbol of the Divine is to miss out on its significance altogether. An eternal song of the Divine, Aum is the mysterious cosmic energy that is the substratum of all things and all beings of the entire universe.

Aum is the very essence of everything that is sacred in Hindu thought. Aum forms the first letter of most Vedic mantras. The word has other connotations too. It is the diadem of Hinduism, and an invaluable gift of the Aryans to humanity.

47

The Swastika Symbolizes the Well-being of All

The symbol of swastika has been used by Indians since time immemorial. It is a historical and sacred symbol in several Indian religions. According to archaeological records, it first appeared around 2500 BC in the Indus Valley Civilization. It rose to greater importance in Buddhism during the time of the Mauryan Empire. Swastika is one of the 108 symbols of Lord Vishnu, and represents the sun's rays, upon which life depends. Its use as sun's symbol can be seen in its representation of the sun god, Surya. An emblem pointing in all the four directions, it signifies grounded stability and is used in most Hindu *yantra*s, religious designs, and during rituals. In Hindu sacred texts, the four sides of the symbol denote the four *purusharthas*, the four Vedas, the four varnas, the four dhams, the four ashrams or stages of life and the four gods— Brahma, Vishnu, Mahesh and Ganesh.

The word 'swastika' originates from the Sanskrit words *swa* and *asti*, meaning 'good luck' and 'well-being'. The word has other connotations as well, such as good wishes, blessings and good deeds. In Vedic literature, there are *swastipatha* known as *swastivachan*, which are to be recited on auspicious occasions. The symbol is chiefly used for well-being—shubha—and wealth—labha—by the Indian business community. Swastika is used by Hindus as well as Jains since ancient times.

It is not just a religious symbol but also a potent scientific ensign that encompasses the secrets of Mother Nature, and has the potency to draw divine power from the twenty-seven nakshatras or constellations and disperse it around. However, to obtain the desired result, this symbol has to be drawn with a special mixture of Gangajal, *gomutra* or cow's urine, kumkum, turmeric and saffron. All these ingredients have disinfecting properties and are sacred and vibrant. For drawing the symbol in the traditional manner, one has to first draw a line from east to west; then crossing this line in the centre, another line is to be drawn from north to south. After this, the symbol is to be drawn clockwise (as per the law of nature, the present moves to the future clockwise). The traditionally drawn swastika does not remain a mere symbol; it becomes an enlivened emblem that emanates divine vibrations for well-being. Sadly, today we draw this auspicious sign with chemically made kumkum and other unholy substances. No wonder the symbol seldom gives the desired result, because we do not observe the traditional science behind it; rather, we treat it as a mere religious routine.

Jainism also accords a great deal of prominence to the swastika. It is a symbol of the seventh *jina* or saint, Tirthankara Suparsva. In the *Shwetambar* Jain tradition, it is also one of the symbols of the ashta *mangala*s representing the eight well-beings. It is considered one of the twenty-four auspicious marks and the emblem of the seventh *arhat* of the present age. All Jain temples and holy books must contain the swastika, and ceremonies typically begin and end by creating a swastika mark several times with rice around the altar. Jains use rice to make a swastika—also known as *sathiyo* or *sathiya* in Gujarat—in front of statues in their temples. They put an offering on this swastika, usually a ripe or dried fruit, a sweet, and a coin or currency note. According to Jain thought, the four sides of the symbol represent the four stages of reincarnation. Interestingly, this ancient symbol is also widely used by rural people of India in their folk art.

The swastika symbol is believed to have been stamped on Gautama Buddha's chest by his initiates after his death. It is known as 'The Heart's Seal'. The swastika also figures on the pillars built by Ashoka. With the Silk Route transmission of Buddhism, the Buddhist swastika spread to Tibet and China. The swastika marks the beginning of many Buddhist scriptures, similar to Jain holy books. It appears on the chest of some statues of Gautama Buddha and is often incised on the soles of the feet of the Buddha in statuary.

Surprisingly, swastika is one of the most common symbols used in the world. A gold necklace with three swastika images found at Marlik in Iran dates back to the first millennium BC. The Japanese call the swastika *manji*. In Japan, Korea and Taiwan, tourist maps use this symbol to denote a temple. The swastika is widely used in Buddhist temples in China. In fact, the symbol is commonly associated with Buddhism the world over.

In some parts of the Western world, this auspicious emblem is regarded as a 'Hate Symbol'. Nazi Germany had adopted the swastika as its official emblem in 1935 under the leadership of Adolf Hitler. Modern Jews abhor the swastika as it is associated with the Nazis who committed inhuman atrocities against them during World War II.

In India and Nepal, electoral ballot papers are stamped with a round swastika-like pattern to ensure that the accidental ink imprint on the other side of a folded ballot paper can be correctly identified as such. Many business and other organizations such as the Ahmedabad Stock Exchange and the Nepal Chamber of Commerce have adopted the swastika as their logos.

48

Sanskrit: A Language of Scientific Sounds

अ आ इ ई उ ऊ

ए ऐ ओ औ

ऋ ॠ ऌ अं अः

क ख ग घ ङ

च छ ज झ ञ

ट ठ ड ढ ण

त थ द ध न

प फ ब भ म

य र ल व

श ष स ह

According to the *Shabda Brahma*, everything subtle or gross originates in sound. The ancient authoritative sources on Yoga hold the view that there are fifty distinct mother vibrations in this universe called the *matrika*, which were revealed to celebrated yogis and rishis of the past during their state of deep contemplation. These rishis, on the basis of *vacha* tatwa or phonetic principle, formulated a language with the basic fifty mother vibrations and named it Sanskrit, meaning 'the refined'. According to Hindu mythology, Vacha, the goddess of speech, invented the language. Another view is that the language was the result of the amalgam of the Indus and the Aryan peoples. According to yet another view, the word 'Sanskrit' comes from 'Sans-kit', one that hones or refines, which is meant for development of knowledge. Of all languages, Sanskrit is the most direct way to approach the transient state to gain knowledge.

Since Sanskrit letters are closest to mother vibrations, the language is rightly claimed to be the most scientific, and it is spiritual in character as well. When properly pronounced, Sanskrit penetrates into the deepest level of our mind. There are languages that are musical and lyrical to the ear but touch only the upper layer of our mind, whereas Sanskrit strikes a chord within, in the innermost core of the mind. Sanskrit is the only language that makes effective use of the throat, teeth, palate, tongue and lips to produce a wide range of sounds that its alphabet demands. Unlike English, Sanskrit, which is read as it is written, has fifty-one alphabets in the Devanagari script.

When a man pronounces letters of the Sanskrit alphabet correctly, it leaves a very positive effect on his body and mind. Moreover, it equally impacts those who listen to its correct pronunciation. This was the reason why it was believed in ancient India that whoever simply listened to the scriptures, attained enlightenment. Correct pronunciation of each Vedic syllable or letter along with the proper accent is absolutely essential. The sound of mantras reaches our ears in two ways: as vibrations of ether, and as vibrations of air. Vibrations of ether cannot be perceived in the physical sense by ordinary human beings. However, the second type of sound can be easily heard since it is audible. Sanskrit has the latent power to produce both types of vibrations.

Till the Gupta period, Sanskrit was the language of the land; thereafter it gradually died. However, a survey conducted by the Anthropological Survey of India has revealed a resurgence of Sanskrit in recent years (*India Year Book*, Publications Division, Government of India, 2003). Once considered almost extinct as a spoken language, Sanskrit is now the mother tongue of some 6,000 people in India. There are five Sanskrit universities in the country. Doordarshan, the national television channel, too is doing its bit to popularize the language: it offers Sanskrit news bulletins in an effort to revive the language. During the swearing-in ceremony of newly elected members of Parliament, a few members take their oaths in Sanskrit.

According to a Varanasi-based Sanskrit scholar, pop diva Madonna once desired to undergo a one-week crash course to hone her Sanskrit pronunciation (*Times of India*). She was convinced that correctly pronounced Sanskrit has twice the impact on listeners.

49

Why Does the Sound of Temple Bell and Gong Flush Out Negativity?

Ancient Indian wise men discovered long ago that rhythmic sound works as an effective cleanser of negativity and restores energies. Therefore, ringing of the temple bell and gong at the time of arati in the morning and evening was made an integral part of daily rituals in temples.

Though some people go to temples to offer their pure selfless prayer, most visit temples to seek solace for their grieving, hard times, mental agony, diseases or the unrest in their hearts. After their prayers, when leaving for their homes, they leave behind a lot of negativity in the temple area. Therefore, regular cleansing of the temple space is done twice daily at sunrise and sunset by ringing the bell and gong together with blowing of the conch. In south Indian temples it is done through music. There, at the time of arati, *nadaswaram* and drums are played.

Collective chanting of mantras aloud, reciting names of gods and singing their bhajans also help to restore the lost energy of the temple space. In homes, it can be achieved by playing a CD of healing mantras, ringing of bell, or using singing bowls particularly in corners where negativity harbours the most. This helps immensely in creating good vibes and in driving negativity out of the walls of a house. Rhythmic sound is the best way to flush out negative energies from any sick structure. It is often experienced that one feels uncomfortable and uneasy when one goes to such a house where prolonged illness has existed or to a hospital where diseases have a natural dwelling, or to a police station, where negative thoughts and emotions find an abode. In these places negativity enters deep and gets accumulated in their walls. Regular and sustained clearing of such places by playing soothing music helps replenish their sapped out energy.

Besides sound, light and air also work as uplifters of positive chi. Most traditional temples are built facing the east for natural light. Burning of incense sticks also purifies space. That is why *dhoopbatti* and *agarbatti* are lit in temples and homes.

50

The Vedas and Puranas

The Vedas and Puranas are often referred to together, but in fact they belong to two different ages. The Vedas—four in number—are the oldest written text whereas the Puranas—eighteen in number—came much later. Moreover, the subject matter that they deal with is also different. The Vedas contain knowledge of the cosmos and the universe around us, as revealed directly by the Supreme Lord to ancient saints and seers while they were in deep meditation, during the *Satya Yuga* when man was in total harmony with nature. The basic elements, the panchabhootas, were then in perfect balance. The seasons turned from one to the other with precision. The Vedic society was well organized, people were spartan and disciplined, and life was simple, smooth, and free from stress and mental turmoil. Human thoughts were pure and well meaning, and the power of spoken words was at its best: what was uttered with intent came true. The concept of ashirwad or blessings and *shrap* or curse was in vogue. It is for this reason that no avatar took birth during the time when the Vedas were revealed to the rishis. The Vedic gods represented the forces of nature, such as Agni, Vayu, Varuna and Indra. It is, however, difficult to date the Vedas as they were passed on orally for thousands of years before being finally penned.

It was during the Vedic era that the first organized Aryan society was established. Social customs and traditions were framed. Duties and responsibilities of all members of society were laid down and tenets for a happy family were spelt out.

The Vedas contain hymns and mantras whereas the Puranas relate stories about original clans, kings and the people they ruled, together with details of the society they lived in. Both the Indian epics, the Ramayana and the Mahabharata, belong to the Puranic age. The Puranic gods are Vishnu, Shiva, Brahma, Durga, Ganesh, Hanuman and so on. Vishnu's avatars — Vamana, Narasimha, Rama and Krishna — took birth during the Puranic age.

The knowledge contained in the Vedas is objective and definitive whereas the content of the Puranas is philosophical and subjective. The school of tantra, the text of Vedic rituals, came about in the Puranic age; no tantra existed in the Vedic age.

It was during the Puranic age that man began to drift away from nature; his life was no longer as pure as it had been during the Satya Yuga. His thoughts became impure and egoistic. The balance of the elements was lost; hence, there was a need to save mankind, for which Lord Vishnu reincarnated to balance the equilibrium.

51

The Science of Mantras

ॐ तर्यम्बकम् यजामहे सुगन्धिम् पुष्टिविर्धनम् ।
ऊर्वारुकमिव बन्धनान् मृत्योर्मुक्षीय मामरतात् ॥

Om trayambakam yajaamahe sugandhim pushtivardhanam
Urvaarukamiva bandhanaan mrityor muksheeya maamritaat

A mantra is basically a sound formula that is carefully formed by stringing together certain selected primordial vibrations or *bija*, which, when properly pronounced, are capable of activating the elements of Mother Nature. When activated through japa or repetition, a mantra gives rise to a distinct vibration. The rishis who devised mantras were called *mantradrastar*. Rishi Vishwamitra was the mantradrastaar of the sacred Gayatri Mantra, and sage Vashishtha was the mantradrastaar of the life-protecting *maha mrityunjaya* mantra. The purpose behind reciting a mantra is to free your mind of all redundant and evil thoughts. In Sanskrit, *mann* means 'mind' and *tra* means 'freeing'. So, a mantra is a means to cleanse our mind of negative thoughts. Before formulating a mantra, its originator would select each of its letters with great deliberation, and experiment its effects on himself before offering it to society. A mantra becomes potent only when concentrated upon, and when the presiding deity of the mantra is invoked, manifested, and pleased with the sincere efforts of the devotee.

Aum is a monosyllable, therefore, it is an *ekakshara* mantra. The well-known mantra *Om namah Shivaya* is a *panchakshara* mantra, with five syllables, whereas *Om Namo Bhagavatey Vasudevaya* is a *dwadashakshara* mantra, with twelve syllables. Further, the mantras that are found in the Vedas are known as Vedic mantras, while the others are general mantras, but they too are equally potent. Vedic mantras are not only rich in their meaning, but also in the sound emanating from their accurate chanting. In the *Agni Purana*, Agnidev, the god of fire, classifies mantras and says that mantras with more than twenty syllables are called *mahamantras*, and usually end with *swaha* or *namah*. Mantras that end with swaha remove diseases and problems and bring peace in one's life. Mantras that end with namah are used to attract wealth, prosperity and fame. Besides, there are mantras that carry the sound *futt* at the end: these are very harsh and carry destructive powers for any problem or enemy.

To activate the power of a mantra, mere repetition is not enough. During the course of sadhana of a mantra, one has to conserve one's energy to its maximum by observing celibacy, controlling anger and minimum use of speech. In our modern-day life, it is not possible to observe these religious tenets. No wonder, mantras do not yield the desired result. Moreover, before mastering a mantra, one is required to repeat it with full concentration for a specific number of times, maybe over a lakh times.

Also, a particular mantra, while fruitful for one may not necessarily be efficacious for another. Which mantra would suit whom depends upon the spiritual level of the seeker. However, there are certain universal mantras like the Gayatri Mantra, which can be recited by all. For fruitful results, a mantra should be properly seeded by a competent guru. Another interesting fact about mantras is that when these are recited during an eclipse, their efficacy is enhanced manifold. The science behind this belief is that during an eclipse, the upward gravitational pull is augmented and the sound energy that one releases by repeating the mantra goes to the astral world faster than on normal days.

One should remember that if mantras are translated into any other language, their sound vibrations would be lost because they will have different sound wavelengths. For a mantra to be effective in the shortest time, it is mandatory for the seeker to do mantra japa at the same place, same time, on the same *asana* or seat, with the same rosary, and while facing the same direction.

It is interesting to note that Dr Howard Steingeril, an American scientist, has established in his physiology laboratory that recitation of the Gayatri Mantra produces 1,10,000 harmonious sound waves per second ('The Best Divine Prayer/Hymn in the World', December 2012). Similarly, other mantras also produce sound waves and bestow spiritual strength upon their chanter who receives supernatural powers.

In ancient days, when idols of deities for temples were carved out of rocks, the sculptor would mentally recite the mantra associated with the deity. Not only that, he would also refrain from any sort of mental chatter or distraction while repeating the mantras. Idols thus carved were enlivened due to the power of the mantras. In Ayurveda, certain medicines were divinized before being administered, by reciting a mantra. Gemstones were also empowered prior to their being set into a ring or an amulet. During the epic days, arrows were shot at an adversary after reciting a mantra and naming the enemy. In this way, they were similar to the modern-day guided missiles. *Lakshmana rekha*, which Lakshmana drew before leaving Sita in the *kuti* or hut at Panchavati, was charged with the power of a mantra, which would protect Sita from harm, as long as she stayed within the circle. Even Ravana was unable to cross over the mantra circle drawn by Lakshmana around the hut. Such was the power of mantras.

The science behind all these old practices was to infuse nature's invisible subtle energy into visible objects such as idols, arrows, gems and medicines, and divinize them.

52
Yoga—The Science of Vital Breath

The word 'yoga' has many meanings, but the most accepted one is 'to unite' or 'to yoke' the mind with the spirit. It is derived from the Sanskrit root '*yuj*', which means 'to cause union of mind, body and soul'. Someone who sincerely practises yoga and follows its philosophy is called a yogi or yogin. Yoga is essentially associated with meditation practices.

Yoga is universal and does not belong to any one particular religion or sect. It refers to traditional physical, mental and spiritual disciplines involving body exercises, controlled breathing and emotional restrain. Sage Patanjali is widely regarded as the father of yoga, and mythologically, Shiva, the god of destruction, is associated with yoga. One of the seals excavated from the sites of the Indus Valley Civilization confirms this fact, wherein Shiva as Pashupati is seen seated in a *Yogamudra* or posture. Patanjali, through his work, *Yoga Sutra*, which has fifty-eight sutras, made available to seekers this ancient science and art of balanced breathing and meditation. Patanjali was so named because he descended in the form of a *pata* or small snake into Panini's *anjali* or palm.

A healthy body is the principal means of acquiring virtue, wealth and liberation. Yoga increases and harmonizes our level of prana or vital energy through balanced breathing which is essential for holistic health. All food articles also have prana, and so yoga stresses on the right type of food as well.

Our thought process consumes a considerable amount of our prana, with negative thoughts heading the list. Hence, yoga advocates positive thoughts and avoiding ill thinking. The more prana you have, the more vitality you have. If you have a balanced prana, you will be healthy, alert and enthusiastic. But when prana is depleted, you will age and be prone to diseases. Yoga is the panacea for all such ills of man and through yoga, our body cells experience rejuvenation. Interestingly, Jainism defines yoga as the sum total of all activities of mind, speech and body.

In Western countries (even in our own country nowadays), fatigue, exhaustion and nervous depressions are frequently experienced. Psychiatrists and counsellors have their hands full because more and more people become victims of anxieties, complexes and inhibitions. They feel torn apart due to the stress of life and strained personal relations. Although it has taken many years, yoga has become immensely popular in the West as people have benefitted from it. As yoga integrates mind-body-soul, it enables people to calm their inner turmoil, which in turn reduces stress and encourages peace and harmony in all aspects of life.

Yoga bestows divine sight with which we are able to resolve not only our gross worldly problems, but also gain knowledge about our life beyond. This is because with yogic power, mental strength enhances manifold. Yoga is a wonderful system that helps one to acquire patience, calm and self-control; it teaches concentration and develops attention. No wonder yoga is now hailed the world over.

However, there are people for whom yoga is nothing more than certain twisted physical postures and acrobatic feats. Unfortunately, it has become a mere tool for some figure-conscious sections of our society to keep slim and trim. They attend yoga classes not to improve their life but to make a fashion statement and widen their social circle. True yoga and its tenets, *yama niyamas*, as laid down by sage Patanjali, hold no meaning for them. In fact, the yoga gurus who conduct such classes are themselves unaware of the principles and theory behind each yoga posture. For these gurus, yoga is a mere means to earn quick and easy money from people who want a size-zero figure.

Real yoga not only improves one on the physical plane but also improves one spiritually. It is the science of soul whose goal is attainment of a state of spiritual insight and inner tranquillity through a healthy body that consciously breathes in vital energy.

53

Why Is the Cow Revered?

The cow has been revered in India since ancient days. Hindu scriptures describe the cow as the mother of the whole universe. She finds mention in all Hindu scriptures—the Vedas, Puranas, Ramayana, Mahabharata and others. The Vedas assert that all objects of the world, be they animate or inanimate, have divine elements of only one deity, whereas the cow has the essentials of all the gods. The cow, therefore, has been described as the amalgam of all gods and goddesses. The Puranas mention several divine cows such as Kamadhenu, Nandini, Surabhi, Kapila, Subhadra and Bahula. In fact, these names belong to different breeds of cows that existed during Puranic days.

Ancient sages and seers studied nature and animals in depth. They found that the cow and its milk had certain unparalleled characteristics and properties that were immensely useful for man. Hence, the cow was accorded sanctity. There are other reasons too that make the cow different from other animals.

According to the Vedas, the cow is *aghnya*, which means 'not to be killed'. It was considered the most valuable possession of the Aryans. Cows' urine contains ammonia which is antiseptic, while its milk is nearest to mother's milk. Hence, it is recommended for infants as it has a good quantity of lactose that enables infants to fight diseases. Cow milk contains about 87 per cent water and 4 per cent fat. It has less sugar, more salts, and four times as much casein—an important protein— as human milk. However, cow milk may vary greatly, depending on the breed, the health of the individual cow, and the time between milk extractions. The last milk to be drawn at each milking is richer than the rest. However, the first milk called colostrum helps build the immune system. According to Indian scientists, the red cows' (Kapila) and black-skinned cows' milk has diverse properties in comparison to the white cow's milk because the red and black-skinned cows absorb the rays of the sun differently and this affects the quality of milk.

Cow milk awakens and augments our latent satvik — pure and divine — virtues whereas buffalo milk induces tamasik — inertia and passion — tendencies. This was the prime reason why gods preferred cow milk and its products over buffalo milk, which was favoured by asuras and rakshasas. It is commonly seen that two cow calves can happily stay together whereas two buffalo calves often quarrel — a demonic tendency. It is noteworthy that while Aryans always prided in owning cows, non-Aryans preferred buffaloes as the quantity of milk was more than that from cows.

Cows' milk, curd, ghee, its dung and urine, all are considered sacred. A combination of these five is called *panchagavya*; it is used to mitigate one's sins. The seed of the bel (wood apple) tree, which is dear to Lord Shiva, is believed to have been born of cows' dung. This tree is the abode of Goddess Lakshmi, which is why it is also called *shrivriksha*. Similarly, the original seeds of the blue and pink lotus are also born from cow dung, while *gugal*, an aromatic substance, is obtained from cows' urine and is offered in the havan kund fire to please gods and goddesses. (Source: *Science of Spirituality*, Sanatan Bharatiya Sanskriti Sansthan, Sanatan Santha, Varanasi, November 2005). *Gorochan*, yet another substance which is used for writing mantras and is of saffron colour, is obtained from the cows' horn. An extremely sacred substance, it is used for ritualistic writings and mantras. Thus, everything born of the cow is sacred and compatible with the human system.

Nature has so made the anatomy of the cow that everything born of this unique animal is useful to mankind. The cows' skin is sensitive and receptive to the sun's rays. In the olden days, whenever, any epidemic broke out in a village, all houses were circled with a 4-inch-wide boundary made of cow dung to prevent harmful bacteria from entering the living space. It has been found that if the floor of a house is covered with cow dung paste, it remains free from all harmful bacteria as cow dung contains phosphorous. In fact, it is more effective than most modern disinfectants.

Similarly, cows' urine is also believed to be a disinfectant. If used and consumed with due care, it can cure a number of ailments. Hindu scriptures hold the view that cows' urine is as sacred as Gangajal. That is why it is sprinkled over objects and places of worship to purify and disinfect them. A Kanpur-based medical firm has obtained a US patent for the purpose of using cows' urine as medicine (*Times of India*). In Ayurveda, its many medical uses have been described. According to an old belief, if cow dung is kept in a tuberculosis (TB) sanatorium, it will destroy the TB bacteria therein and cleanse the place.

Many skin and blood disorders are cured by using cow dung and cow urine. In fact, these days, certain modern ashrams have started manufacturing soap and agarbattis or incense sticks from cow dung.

These facts about the cow are scientific and not based on mere myth. If you observe the cow grazing in its natural surroundings, particularly in a jungle, you will see that its selection of grass and plants is different from that of other cattle. It grazes on vegetation that is agreeable to the human system. Even the anatomy of the cow is such that its milk best suits the human body. (Source: *Rishabh Shree*, New Delhi, July–December 1992). The hump of an Indian cow is special, and differs from the small hump seen in Western cows. The skin of Indian cows is also much softer than that of Western cows. However, these attributes are not true in the case of Jersey cows because the genetic mutation of the Jersey cow is different from that of the native cow.

It is, however, unfortunate that cows nowadays are seen grazing on any rubbish lying on the roads and streets, including waste paper and polythene bags. With such fodder to eat, how can the present-day cow live up to its ancient glory?

Why Is Cows' Ghee Significant in Vedic Rituals?
In most Sanatana rituals, ghee is an indispensable component. Ancient scriptures prescribed ghee from cow milk only for ceremonies and religious events. What is so special about cows' ghee that it ranks the best?

Vedic scientists conducted in-depth research on different burning substances and found cows' ghee to be most agreeable to the human system and least harmful to the environment. Hence, they rated it highest in quality and unequal in efficacy. In ancient times, experiments were carried out to verify the truth about this variety of ghee. (Source: *Gobharati*, Cuttack, Odisha, April 2011). Lamps filled with different types of oils and ghee such as mustard oil, coconut oil, linseed oil, kerosene oil, buffaloes' ghee, goats' ghee, etc., were placed in separate closed rooms. In each of these rooms, a man was made to sit facing the lamp and asked to concentrate on the burning wick. It was observed that sooner or later, the eyes of each participant started smarting and tears rolled down their cheeks, except the eyes of the person who sat before the lamp filled with cows' ghee. On the contrary, he experienced coolness in his eyes. This is because the smoke emitted from other lamps contained chemical substances that hurt the eyes and caused irritation, but not the lamp that had cows' ghee. This truth was discovered thousands of years ago by the rishis and munis of India. Moreover, cows' ghee, when burnt, purifies the atmosphere. Such experiments are conducted in Shanti Kunj, an ashram in Haridwar, which is exclusively devoted to such research work. Besides, there is a centre in Pune, Vedic Science Institute, that conducts similar research work. That is why during havans, only cows' ghee used to be poured into the holy fire.

However, the most startling truth related to cows' ghee is that its emission protects the earth from atomic radiations. This property is due to the fact that cows' skin is very sensitive to the suns' rays and absorbs it in such a way that its milk is vitalized and the ghee made from it naturally turns it potent enough to provide protection against radiation. According to Dr Shirowich, a Russian scientist, the cow provides protection from atomic radiation and, hence, houses that have floors plastered with cow dung enjoy protection from radiation (*Reader's Digest*). When ghee made from cows' milk is put into fire, its smoke lessens the ill effects of atomic radiation to a great extent. These are accepted scientific truths (Source: *Spiritual Science*, December 2010, Jodhpur) about the cow, and must be taken into account by the modern generation. Scientists are now working on the use of colostrum in cows' milk against HIV and H1N1. These were the scientific reasons why rishis and munis made cows' ghee an integral part of Sanatan rituals (Source: Vedic Science Institute, Pune, August 2006).

Cow Dung, a Wonderful Substance

Ancient Indian society was purely pastoral and domesticated several animals. The cow was the most favoured. Rishis and munis found that cow dung was a wonder substance, the most wondrous fact about cow dung being that it is a non-conductor of electricity. If lightning strikes a heap of cow dung, it absorbs the electrical energy instantly and does not allow it to enter the earth.

K.V. Singh

In Ayurveda, cow dung is widely used in the treatment of leprosy and monkey bite. In the case of the latter, it gives instant relief to the victim. Likewise, cow dung is useful in treating skin disorders like pimples and it also purifies blood. Soaps made of cow dung are now available in the market and those suffering from skin problems claim to have benefitted from them.

Biogas plants are more eco-friendly in comparison to other gases. The smoke emitted from burning cow dung cakes controls pollution and kills harmful insects. Experts also opine that rubbing cow dung ash on our body regulates and controls blood pressure. It is somewhat unfortunate that in modern society, cow dung has little place in our lifestyle.

54

Why Are There 108 Beads in a Mala or Rosary?

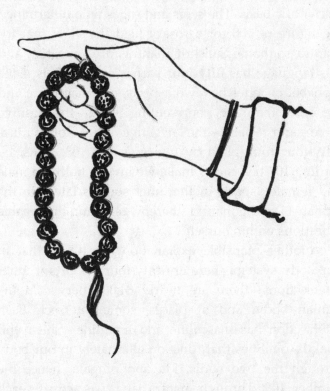

The mala or rosary is used as an aid or a tool to say prayers and repeat God's name not only by Hindus but by other communities as well. Most Hindus use a rosary with 108 beads. This specific number has been considered sacred since time immemorial and is explained in many different ways. The top bead is called the *meru* and is not counted. The turning of the mala commences and concludes at the meru. The figure of 108 for the Hindu rosary is not casual, but has a scientific basis. The seers and sages who determined the figure of 108 for a rosary held the view that for mantra sadhana, Sanskrit mantras are repeated, and this language has fifty-four varnas or alphabets. Each alphabet or letter has two aspects, one masculine and the other feminine, representing Shiva—the positive force—and Shakti—the negative force—of nature. Fifty-four multiplied by two gives us 108. Thus, by turning 108 beads of a mala, we invoke both the male and female aspects of the inner sounds latent in the alphabets of the mantra, thereby generating agreeable vibrations within ourself.

Another plausible explanation for 108 is that in our body system, there are fifty-four important inner intersections—there are nearly 84,000 nerves in the human body, and at places, some intersect. Each intersection has masculine and feminine—Shiva and Shakti—qualities that function alternately in our body through the two nadis, ida and pingala, hence the number 108. Through mantra japa, we activate each intersection of our body, without being conscious of it.

Yet another explanation is that the 108 beads symbolize the 108 elements that constitute the universe. The sun is the pivot of the universe. Any orbit in space has 360 degrees which, when converted into minutes would be 360 x 60 = 21,600. The sun remains for half a year on each side, alternately in the northern and southern *ayana* or declination. When we divide the sum total of minutes into two parts, we get 10,800 minutes. For purity of counting, the zeros are removed and we get the figure of 108.

According to the Indian system of reckoning time, a day of twenty-four hours has sixty *ghati*s, a division of time according to Indian system. Each ghati has sixty *pala*s and each pala has sixty *vipala*s. Thus, in a day, there are 2,16,000 vipalas (60 x 60 x 60 = 2,16,000), which when divided by two, give 1,08,000 vipalas for the day and 1,08,000 vipalas for the night. On removing the zeros, one gets the figure of 108.

Further, the seers of ancient India laid down the number of beads for different types of japas. They prescribed a rosary of twenty-five beads for attaining salvation, a rosary of thirty beads for acquiring wealth, and a rosary of twenty-seven beads for accomplishing very personal desires. However, for all-round well-being, a 108-bead rosary has been specified. Mediums used to make rosaries are tulsi stem, sandalwood, *rudraksha*, *vaijanti* seeds, pearls, turmeric and corals. Each of these is used for a specific purpose. Their use generates different vibes in the body, depending on the type of beads used. Turmeric mala is very useful for performing special prayers for overpowering enemies and to cure jaundice. Other malas too have their special uses.

It is important to know that there is a definite way of using a mala. It is put on the middle finger of the right hand, and with the help of the thumb, each bead of the mala is pulled towards the body. The friction thus caused enlivens the inner intersections of our body to benefit us.

Tasbi, the rosary used by Muslims, has 100 beads interspersed with a *zamin*, a special bead for pause while turning the rosary, after every thirty-three beads and an *imam* on top like the Meru in the Hindu mala. In a Christian rosary, there are sixty beads and a crucifix, while a devout Sikh turns a small rosary with twenty-seven beads as well as one with 108 beads.

Rudraksha Beads: Energy Capsules

The beads of the rudraksha have held great significance in Hindu thought since time immemorial.Rudraksha is the seed of the fruit of the rudraksha tree — *Elacocarpus garniture*. It is covered by a blue outer shell and on ripening, it is called blueberry. Rudraksha trees are primarily grown in Nepal, India, Indonesia and Malaysia.

Rudrakshas may be considered wonder seeds of nature as they are endowed with mystic and divine powers and properties. Rudraksha malas are regarded sacred and powerful, with astrological and health benefits. It is believed that one who wears rudraksha — a single bead or a mala—is untouched by sins, and is protected from all impious deeds and thoughts.

Rudraksha has its etymological origin in the Sanskrit words *rudra* and *aksha*. 'Rudra' is another name for Lord Shiva, and 'aksha' means 'teardrops'. Mythology has it that the rudraksha plant was born out of Lord Shiva's teardrops; in other words, the rudraksha is associated with Shiva, who is the incarnation of well-being. This bead has the power to conquer fear, including the fear of death. This property is singularly responsible for controlling stress and bringing peace, stability and serenity. It is no wonder that for thousands of years, sages and saints of India have adorned their bodies with rudraksha malas, which would enable them to lead fearless lives in far-flung frontiers and lofty mountains.

Rishi Jabal, an ancient sage, belonged to the Bhaskara sect and was the official sanyasi vaidya—a doctor who had renounced the material world—in the royal court of the King of Kashi (presnt-day Varanasi). He carried out extensive research on the rudraksha and authored the *Jabalopanishad*. Sage Jabal spread the knowledge of rudraksha through his disciples. The sage's treatment was primarily based on the rudraksha, and its usage soon became popular among the rich as well as the commoners. Since sage Jabal was a sanyasi, the rudraksha was linked to sanyasis who zealously patronized this wonder seed.

The rudraksha, however, is also for those who pursue worldly life. According to Ayurveda, wearing the rudraksha has a positive effect on the heart and nerves of the wearer. People with high blood pressure benefit from the use of these miracle seeds. Also known for relieving stress, anxiety, depression and other mental ailments, the rudraksha has anti-ageing effects as well. It has also been proved that the rudraksha possesses memory enhancement properties. Some scientists have concluded that the rudraksha mala serves as a safety valve, which absorbs all negative energy and protects its wearer (Source: Rudraline, Mumbai).

In modern times, a great deal of research has been carried out, mostly outside India, to learn more about the rudraksha and its effects on the human body. John Ganet, a British officer, collected a lot of useful information from ancient Indian texts on the rudraksha in 1864. Recently, Dr Abraham Jajuar, an American, undertook extensive work on the medical properties of rudraksha and concluded that it impacts the mental process and cures mental disorders very effectively. Similarly, the University of Cologne (Germany), International University at Miami, Florida, as well as a university in Switzerland carried out comprehensive work to reveal the scientific explanation for the magnetic and other effects such as curing of blood pressure ailments, stress, etc., of rudraksha on the human body. Common conclusions made in these studies are that the rudraksha has electromagnetic, paramagnetic and inductive properties which vary from one *mukhi* or facet to the other. It has been established that rudraksha has electromagnetic power of seven millivolts, which is equal to what is found in most human bodies. These researches also state that when doing japa, if a devotee touches the rudraksha beads—however light that contact maybe—specific electrical impulses are sent to brain centres that transfer information. Thus, these studies of recent years confirm all that sage Jabal had penned in his *Jabalopanishad,* as well as what is mentioned in ancient Indian scriptures.

Ancient scriptures have classified rudraksha beads on the basis of the number of *mukha*s—the natural clefts and furrows they have on their surface. According to the *Jabalopanishad,* each bead has a different effect on the wearer, depending on the number of mukhas it has.

55

Why Should Hindus Not Despise Others?

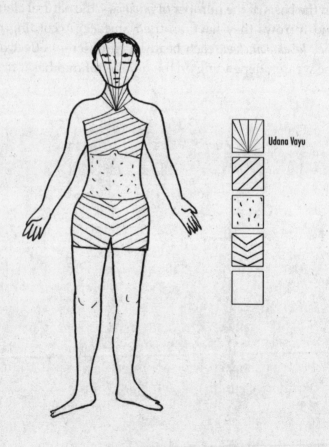

Udana Vayu

Ancient scriptures say that one must not despise others. Behind this religious principle lies the science of acoustics according to which every word has latent power, i.e., when we speak, our words travel on air waves and reach the targeted person. The listener conceives the meaning according to his inherent intent. When one flatters a person, the concerned man feels flattered and delighted, and when one scolds someone, the victim feels hurt and humiliated. Thus, through spoken words, we can affect the feeling of others.

According to solar science, there are forty-eight types of winds called vayu or *marut*. Of these, five are found in different parts of the human body and each has a special function to perform. One of the five winds, *udana* vayu, is found in the region of the human mind and its principal function is to generate thoughts in the mind and orally express them. The udana vayu predominantly has fire element in it, the basic characteristic of which is to burn everything that is put into it. Therefore, when one speaks ill of someone, the udana vayu, through its latent fire, burns the sins of the despised person and ironically, adversely affects the person who speaks ill. In this way, when one speaks ill of another man, he is actually hurting and damaging himself. Thus, ancient seers and sages always preached that one must not speak ill of others; because it backfires to return to its originator and harms him.

The practice of confession in Christianity is also based on the principle of udana vayu. Sitting in a confession box, when one sincerely admits to one's sins, it gets burnt due to the effect of udana vayu and the person is saved from the fires of hell.

One of the fundamental truths of nature is that whatever good or bad we do, we are accordingly rewarded or punished. If one does good to others, nature pays back manifold. Similarly, bad actions attract punishment. The adage of 'as your sow, so shall you reap' works on this principle of nature. Keeping an account of good and bad actions is nature's exclusive responsibility. When a man despises someone, he assumes the role of a judge, pronouncing judgements on others' actions. This critical attitude of a man towards the actions of others is interference in nature's design, the consequences of which are always damaging.

In Hindu scriptures, another significant tenet is that one must not reveal one's guru mantra — a mantra ceremoniously received from a holy person — nor should one boast about one's good acts. The principle of udana vayu operates behind these restrictions as the efficacy of the mantra is lost in the telling. Likewise, the merit of good acts is lost in the boasting.

56

Is the Use of Gemstones Scientific or a Myth?

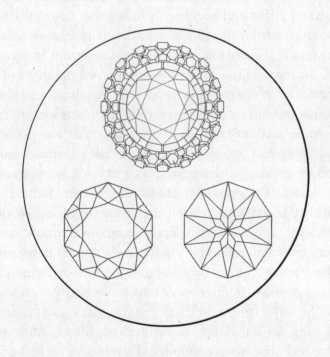

Ancient rishis and munis held that the use of *ratna*s or gemstones exerts great influence on human beings. As objects of purity, these colourful mystical stones counter and balance the malefic effects of planets and stars that affect human life. According to Hindu thought, each gemstone is a highly sensitive radioactive crystal that can filter out specific cosmic rays and colours that have a strong effect on the human body and mind. Modern scientists also confirm this fact. Ancient rishis and munis concluded that ruby attracts vibrations from the sun, pearl attracts vibrations from the moon, the emerald attracts vibrations from Mercury or Budha, yellow sapphire attracts vibrations from Jupiter or Brihaspati, diamond attracts vibrations from Venus or Shukra, and blue sapphire attracts vibrations from Saturn or Shani. Stones are keys that can unlock our potential as human beings. They expand our consciousness, enhance our lives and calm our stresses.

Jewels, when they come in contact with the human body, exert an electromagnetic influence on physical cells. Human body contains carbon and various metallic elements that are also found in jewels. Planetary vibrations continuously exercise an influence on a person through sensory nerves. Secondly, a person might suffer from a deficiency of certain rays or colours causing an imbalance in his system, thus leading to physical diseases or emotional problems or ill luck. Stones, like colours, plants and other natural objects, are magical tools that can bring about transformation in us.

Use of gemstones can compensate for a deficiency by transmitting the required rays and colours into our body and also filter out their negative influences. Muslims and Christians also believe in the use of gems. However, selection of a gem and its setting in a ring or a pendent warrant certain precautions and practices. Without properly 'charging' a gem, it is as good as a piece of stone. Therefore, for a gem to be useful, it has to be first purified and charged with a specific number of appropriate mantras before wearing it. Gems worn without procedure are not that efficacious.

Today, a new awareness about the magical value of stones has swept the present-day world. Stone therapy has been accepted as an alternative medicine. Like the growing use of herbs, the use of stones is also on the rise. Stones are magical batteries that contain and concentrate the earth's energies. They are manifestations of the universal forces of gods, goddesses, deities and fate.

57

Why Should We Not Sleep Facing the South?

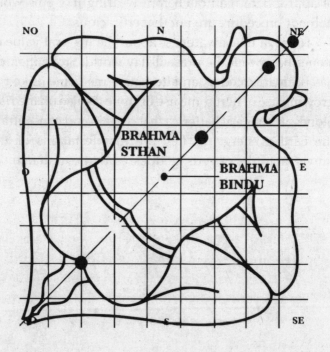

India's great spiritual thinkers, including some Buddhist and Jain scholars, considered the human body as a replica of the entire universe. According to them, our head represents the North Pole and the feet the South. Philosophically, the north is godly, full of light, hope and success; whereas the south is sad, downward, dark, full of despair and death. The north stands for heaven and the south for the region of Death.

According to the scientific theory of magnetic principles, opposite poles attract each other while like poles repel. When we sleep facing the south, our feet will be southwards, and the two poles of the body and the physical world will hence pull apart, which would disturb the natural flow of blood circulation and the digestive system of our body. Food consumed by us will also be adversely affected. Instead of slipping down to the rectum, the natural outlet of our body, it would be pushed upwards towards the heart due to the repelling gravitational pull of the two poles, causing discomfort and distress in the body. Hence, our sleep will be adversely affected because of disturbed blood circulation. If a person continues to sleep facing the south, his health will eventually be affected. According to the tenets of *Vastu Shastra* as well, one must not sleep with feet towards the south.

58

What's in a Name?

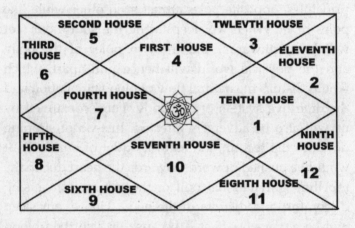

India's ancient scriptures assign great significance to one's name. The name denotes the sound form of a person. According to Hindu sacred books, a person has two forms: physical and sonic. The two have to be in harmony with each other for the good of the person. When the physical form of a man is different from the sonic form, it creates negative effects for him. Therefore, both forms should be compatible. As the saying goes, 'There is a lot in a name.'

Realizing the importance of a name, ancient seers devised a special ceremony—namakaran—to name a newborn within six days of birth. On the birth of a child, his *janma kundali* or birth chart was drawn according to the placement of stars and planets at the time of his birth. The birth chart chalked out thus indicated the letters in the alphabet whose sound waves were in accord with the physical form of the infant. Once the letters were determined by qualified astrologers or gurus, the infant was given a name that was auspicious, well meaning, and appropriate with the first letter of the name being one of the letters determined by the pundit. The science behind the namakaran ceremony was that each time the child would be addressed by his name, the sound form with its latent energy and meaning would accordingly impact the child.

Repeating a name has a definite effect according to the science of acoustics. Good names will have an agreeable effect and bad ones adverse. Names of gods and spiritual names always have a pleasant effect because their physical and sound forms are consistent and non-different. That is why mantras are repeated a thousand times for the desired results. The chanting of gods' names is quite influential because the power of gods is latent in them.

However, in modern society, scant significance is accorded while naming a newborn child. Faniciful names or names without any meaning are given to children. Nowadays, more often than not, we see parents caring little about norms and naming their child as per their whims and fancies. Subsequently, unknown to us, the child faces adversity at every turn of his life. No wonder, people are now seen changing spellings of their names to create vibrations for their success in life.

There was a time when children were named Rama, Krishna, Shravana, Sita, Suneeta, or Geeta. Today, we name them Rocky, Vicky, Babloo or Babli. The fault is of the age we live in. There are hardly any true pundits who can rightly draw a birth chart because the science of naming is more or less lost and defunct.

59
Honey–A Divine Product of Nature

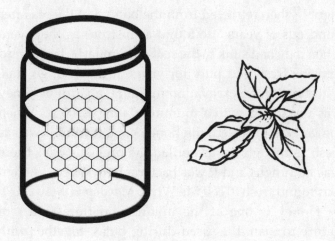

Honey is a divine product of Mother Nature. It is inevitably used in most rituals and pujas, especially while performing the abhisheka or bathing ritual of a deity. According to the original Sanatan philosophy, the best of things are to be offered to the Divine. That is why, people of means offer gold, silk, coconuts and fruits to gods.

Honey enjoys a special place amongst the offerings. Gold is a wonder metal that does not rust or corrode with weather or time. It is seen that gold coins or ingots, when retrieved from the bottom of the sea after hundreds of years, are found as lustrous as they were when they had sunk to the seabed. Similarly, honey also remains fresh and pure for years. It does not go stale with time. In an excavation in Egypt, a jarful of honey was unearthed with a mummy dating 1,500 BC. When the jar was unsealed, the honey contained in it was as fresh as though it was bottled the previous day! There was no fungus and it was bacteria free. When tasted, it was found fresh ('Tell Me Why', *Manorama*, May 2008).

Honey is one of the unique and purest gifts of nature to man. It is used during pujas, together with other wholesome products such as ghee, curd and milk. The reason for honey being so pure is the queer process and technique through which it is produced. Tiny honeybees laboriously collect nectar from flowers and plants and deposit it in the beehive which by itself is a mystic storage. During winters, the honey is solidified and with the onset of summers, it melts to its natural state.

In fact, honeybees do not gather honey from flowers for man to take it out for his consumption. They gather it for their queen bee to maintain her youth and vigour. When man discovered this secret, he used it for his benefit. Physicians to the gods, sages Ashwini Kumaras carried out extensive research on honey and its characteristics. The two sages of the Vedic times successfully used honey to cure ailments and revitalize man's vigour. It may surprise some to know that honey was even used to augment agricultural produce. Before being sown, seeds were soaked in honey and milk, and consequently, the harvest was abundant and the quality of grains was healthy and sweet in taste.

In Ayurveda as well as in allopathy, the use of honey is considered as rejuvenating. It is not surprising to find honey as a 'must have' item on breakfast tables in homes.

According to both ancient scriptures and Ayurveda, the quality and ingredients of honey varied, depending upon the vegetation and flowers from which the bees collected the honey and the season in which it was collected. Honey obtained from flowers of neem tree is considered good for patients with poor digestive system. Honey collected from white flowers looks whitish, while the honey extracted from mustard, mango and saffron flowers is golden in its countenance.

The smell and taste of honey depends on the smell of the majority of flowers and plants from which it has been obtained. Honey extracted in the month of kartika (October–November) is full of medicinal value, but is not

so commonly available. Honey collected by bees during
the months of *phalguna* and chaitra (February–April)
from mustard flowers also has medicinal qualities.
The Himalayan honey turns white after it solidifies;
it develops granules and emanates a gentle smell. On
the other hand, honey collected during *baishakha* and
jyaishtha (April–June) is red in colour and has aromatic
fragrance. The ashadha honey, honey obtained in the
month of June–July, is also red but solidifies quickly. At
times, this honey is somewhat bitter in taste. It is used
for generating heat in the body.

Chemically, honey has 50 per cent glucose and
some fructose and maltose. It also has vitamins A, B,
D and E in sufficient quantities. Besides, iron, calcium,
manganese, sulphur, phosphorus, sodium and iodine
are found in it. Traces of copper with curative properties
are also present in honey. All these put together render
honey bacteria-free. Consumption of honey is good for
enhancement of memory, and particularly invigorates
and rejuvenates those who are engaged in mental
work.

Pure honey does not dissolve by itself when put into
water. To test whether or not honey is pure, pour some
slowly into a glass of water. If it settles down at the
bottom of the glass without dissolving into the water, it
is pure. Another method to verify the purity of honey is
to offer it to a dog. If it is pure, the dog will not consume
it. The more viscose the honey is, the better is its quality.
A point of caution is that honey must not be heated or
else it will turn poisonous. Likewise, honey and ghee of

same weight must not be consumed together. This too is poisonous.

However, honey, ghee, curd, milk and sugar are mixed to prepare *madhuparka* and distributed after puja in temples and homes as prasad.

60

Difference between Sanatana Dharma and Hindu Dharma

Most of us may find it hard to even acknowledge any difference between Sanatana Dharma and Hindu Dharma, yet there is a difference. This is because Hindu Dharma is the present-day name of Sanatana Dharma, which was the original religion of the land. Sanatana Dharma refers to that Vedic period of the Aryans when the first organized society was formed in the country. Rights and responsibilities of every member of society were drawn, developed and expected to be followed. An ultimate aim and purpose of life was set for all to achieve. Self-realization, knowledge of self and accepting the supremacy of the Almighty were the goal of all. The social set-up so developed was divided into different sections according to the vocation they carry out in their lives. The Vedas did exist, but were then unwritten and passed on orally from one generation to the other. Sanatana Dharma was not founded by one, but by many. It was dynamic and a religion of tolerance and acceptance. The trinity of Brahma, Vishnu and Mahesh did not exist then; only the forces of nature and their controlling deities like Vayu, Agni, Varuna and Indra—existed. No temples were seen during the Sanatana era; they appeared later.

During the Sanatana period, man was nearest to nature. The basic elements, the panchabhootas, were in perfect harmony with each other. Seasons turned with precision from one to the other. All human actions and activities were such that maintained the equilibrium of nature. No action of men disturbed the balance between them and nature. Sages of Sanatana Dharma believed that the Supreme Lord is both the cause and the effect. If the universe is the effect, God is the cause.

The power of spoken words was high in the Sanatana era. Human words spoken with clear realization and deep concentration came true as the power of ashirwad or blessings and of shrap or curse.

Sanatana Dharma was based on the Vedas, which were revealed directly to rishis and munis, who contemplated on all aspects and secrets of the cosmos. The knowledge they thus gained was orally handed over to society for its benefit. Its teachings were not confined to any one particular text, but took inspiration from life as revealed to sages. The soul is divine; it is pure, perfect, infinite, part of God, yet independent of Him. It resides in a body but changes it and moves to another. Many of its tenets like the *atma*, *paramatma*, karma, maya and incarnation are unique, which baffle many in the modern age.

It was a pure, unpolluted and original society. Prior to this, no proper social set-up had existed. It is for this reason that no avatar of God descended on earth during this period. The religion that the Aryans then followed was named Sanatana, which means eternal and the earliest.

The name 'Hindu' is not native to the land as it was given to the people of India by Persians when referring to the Aryans who lived beyond the river Sindhu, as the land where they resided was called Hind by them. Hindu, thus, is not a native word of India. It came into being when indigenous people came in contact with other faiths and religions of the world. A multitude of gods and goddess appeared within the Hindu pantheon of deities with time. The trinity of Brahma, Vishnu and Mahesh is the most important, but it belongs to the later era.

By the time the pure Sanatana Aryan society came in contact with other religions of the contemporary world, a lot of changes had taken place within its own social set-up. The original purity of thought and the sincerity and simplicity of action had been considerably lost. Man's ego was evident in his actions and thoughts. Therefore, there was a need to balance the relation between man and nature. No wonder, avatars descended during later stages of the Sanatana society.

On contact with other faiths of the world, our own religion was affected. We adopted some of their traditions and practices, which gradually transformed our society. The changes that took place in our social set-up are now an integral part of our society. It is difficult to recognize which practice or tradition is alien and which is pure Aryan. This reality is well illustrated in the modern-day practice of applying *mehndi* or henna on the palms of a bride at the time of her marriage. This custom is not Indian. We adopted this from Persians and Arabs. In Aryan culture, haldi or turmeric was applied on the bride's palms by her parents at the time of marriage. Similarly, the original form of most of our festivals has also undergone changes. Modern-day religious rituals are no longer original but adopted and transformed. In other words, the transformed pure Sanatana Dharma of yesterday is today's Hindu Dharma with changes that took place with passage of time or due to compulsion of circumstances.

Acknowledgements

I owe the writing of this book to the rare and in-depth knowledge of the great souls, saints and scholars with whom I interacted and discussed from time to time the religious practices, rites and rituals at different places and stages of my extensive All India Service tenure. I bow at their lotus feet, though they are no longer in their mortal being. When they lived, they remained obscure from press and people, and possessed deep insight and knowledge of our ancient culture and vast, rich heritage. They revealed to me the true intent, and the scientific reasons behind various Hindu traditions. On talking to them I realized they had answers to many hitherto unexplained questions related to Hindu rites and rituals.

I am also greatly indebted to Dr Jayant Balaji Athavale for his books on science and spirituality that immensely inspired me whilst penning the book.